In Response To Detroit Urban Survival Training (IG):

"You are legendary." - **DJ Khaled**

"Too good to be true, unbelievable. Great tactical work to be able to outsmart someone that has a gun on you. What the world would like to see is a TV show, and I want to help you with that. We love what you, Dale, are doing and your wife and team."

- Snoop Dog, Rapper & TV Personality

"We at Fox 2 have known Dale for years; now everyone else does. The eyebrows and uniform, now famous."

- Fox 2 News

"He's legit in self-defense and the security game for 26 years. He was also a Paratrooper; he knows what he is talking about."

- Joaquin Buckley, MMA Fighter

Endorsement Quotes:

"The founder of the Threat Management Center conducted a safety training session for our field agents... The survival tactics demonstrated by Commander Dale Brown and his team was a true asset I received positive feedback from the agents during the training and the kudos continued into the following day."

- Joyce Martin, OIG *(Office of Inspector General)*

"The last two years I have witnessed Threat Management working closely with our litigants and to ensure the safety and security of victims of domestic violence. Threat management has in my humble opinion set the standard for leadership and community outreach in the air of shrinking police services and budget cuts cleanly program start management has a positive and example of responsible corporate citizenship.

Threat Management is building a safer community for all and is an indispensable resource to victims of domestic violence in Southeast Michigan."

- Honorable Richard B. Halloran

"I have known instructor Dale Brown for approximately one year. The tactical instructions taught by Instructor Brown has proven extremely useful to Fugitive Operations, with particular regards to its practical, flexibility and avoiding injury whenever possible while not compromising officer safety. Defense tactics learned at Threat Management Center were immediately applicable in the field and have been employed many times by Fugitive Operations personnel with positive results. Additionally, the professionalism demonstrated by Instructor Brown and his staff has been second to none. I highly recommend Dale Brown and Threat Management Centers on both personal and professional levels."

- John Claypoole, Deportation Officer, US Immigration and Customs Enforcement

"Dale Brown and his personnel have become recognizable through their tactical paramilitary uniform and Dale's iconic black hummer. Dale Brown model and lives by his core philosophy of heroic altruism. His personnel are required to routinely protect individuals whose lives have been threatened, such as domestic violence victims, for free regardless of the level of risk. Dale Brown developed his own training system, called Eclectikan, built on a foundation of tactical psychology, law and skill.

That the honorable members of the Detroit city council nearby recognize and acclaim Dale Brown and The Threat Management Center for their exemplary community service and unquestionable courage and unwavering commitment to protecting those most vulnerable in Detroit and the wider region."

- Detroit City Council

"I would like to congratulate you on becoming one of this year's recipients of the Oakland County Domestic Violence Prevention Award. Your efforts exemplify a standard of excellence and compassion that we all aspire to. Without efforts, many victims would continue to feel helpless and alone. Due to your efforts, Oakland County's coordinated community response is stronger than ever. "

- Lisa J. Ortlieb, Co-Chair - OCCCADV, Domestic Violence Section Leader, & Attorney

"Real-Life Hero" - **Dash Radio**

DETROIT

URBAN SURVIVAL

CHRONICLES | PROTECTION SURVIVOR STORIES OF DOMESTIC ABUSE, THEFT, ROBBERY AND VIOLENCE.

COMMANDER DALE C. BROWN

FEATURING STORIES FROM DETROIT THREAT MANAGEMENT CENTER
V.I.P.E.R.S. BODYGUARD PROGRAM

SEVEN
HOUSE MEDIA

www.sabatekle.com
www.7housemedia.com
Copyright © 2022 Dale C. Brown
Cover 7 House Media, LLC

ISBN: 9798218088729
Library of Congress Control Number: 2022917217

Disclaimer:

Neither the publisher nor the author is engaged in rendering professional advice or services to the reader. The ideas, suggestions, and procedures provided in this book are not intended as a substitute for attending the author's school. Neither the publisher nor the author shall be held liable or responsible for any loss or damage allegedly arising from any suggestion or information contained in this book.

Before attempting to replicate anything that is in the book it is requited to take a class by the author.

This work depicts actual events in the life of the author as truthfully as recollection permits. While all persons within are actual individuals, names and identifying characteristics have been changed to respect their privacy.

DEDICATION

In loving memory of my father Robert K. Brown
My dad said I should read books, so instead, I wrote one.

Furthermore, to Deletha Word, without her, I would have never realized the importance of providing education and protection for the public!

CONTENTS

ACKNOWLEDGMENTS

To my loving wife, aka "wifner" (wife partner), because of you, my personal life is full of love and happiness, and my business has survived and thrived to heights I could have never achieved without you!

For my team members, thank you for your many sacrifices and commitment to the safety of others!

- Icon-1
- Bravo-1
- Saber-1
- Delta-7
- Mantis-11
- Lotus-11
- Jaguar-19
- Mantis-25

To Karen Foster-Flisnik, what you did for me will never be forgotten and I want the world to know that you personally helped me as a business mentor but also as a friend and like a great family member. It is because of your trust and willingness to help me I have successfully been able to help thousands of people survive. You donated $3,000 to help me go and protect families during Hurricane Katrina. NO OTHER PERSON, BUSINESS OR ORGANIZATION WAS WILLING TO DONATE a $1!

Thank you, Karen, for your overwhelming support that helped my family and I, personally and helped my organization save many lives!

To Sgt. Pride Johnson, Detroit PD, thank you for the VIPERS acronym, which I got the idea for — from your unit call sign, viper, and also incorporating the VIPERS in advanced FEMA Police Training for 15 years.

To Trooper Walt Crider, thank you for helping to encourage Law Enforcement professionals and the many government and private sector entities to incorporate our training to help save lives for 17 years.

To Wisam Paulus, thank you for allowing me to provide protection against hijackings of your trucks for the past 24 years — which we take great pride in.

To Dr. James Gorman, thank you for your many years of helping to train 100's of students and team members for nearly a decade.

To Jason Moore, thank you for protecting the Secretary of State from a mob of protesters and for training hundreds of men, women and children in Preventive Threat Management.

To Brandon Hunt, thank you for incorporating our training into the Detroit Police Department and training law enforcement and the general public in Preventive Threat Management for many years.

To Paige Erlich, D.U.S.T. would be some other longer acronym if it were not for your advice that specifically stated that D.U.S.T. will be memorable to people and catchy.

Dave Meadows, since the mid 90's you have been a great friend, supporter and one of the reasons I am successful. I will always consider you my brother.

To my daughter, Indira Brown, thank you for being a loving daughter and the light of my life.

To my son, Miles Brown, as my firstborn child, you'll always have a significant place in my heart and one of the most important reasons for the drive for my success. I am proud of you and your aspirations, achievements, and maturity development over the years.

To my step-son, Kenan Ahmic, it has been an honor to help raise you since you were 7 years old. I am proud of the mature young man that you are at age 18 now. I look forward to guiding you in your continued success in life.

To my loving mother, Dr. Gale Northcross, thank you for a great childhood filled with many happy memories. Thank you for being a STRONG U.S. Army Captain who I always admired and respected. Thank you for supporting me as an adult and helping to support my success in life.

To my sister, Dr. Sonya Brown AKA Don King Jr., thank you for recruiting fights with all neighborhood and kids in foreign countries because of you I learned to fight even though it was not right.

To my mother-in-law aka "Nani" thank you for being a great mother-in-law, helping and supporting our success as a family!

"OUR MISSION IS TO MAKE THE WORLD A SAFER
PLACE THROUGH NON-VIOLENCE."

FOREWORD

By Michigan State Trooper Walter Crider (RET.)

Like most midnight shifts, we patrolled the streets and highways of Detroit to enforce the law. As sworn police officers, my partner and I had our favorite proverbial fishing holes that often yielded "good" arrests (the coveted guns, drug money, and dope). We were cruising the Greektown entertainment district when I saw what I thought was an elite SWAT team. The men dressed in tactical military gear were not cops. They were VIPERS (Violence Intervention Protective Emergency Response System). The men walked in unison, yet I couldn't discern a leader. It wasn't until several nights later that I encountered the leader, Commander Dale Brown.

Emerging seemingly out of a cloud from the entrance of the smoke-filled nightclub, Dale Brown appeared like a warrior king surrounded by his VIPERS. The nightclub, colloquially known as the "River Rat," was not for the faint-hearted.

This downtown entertainment venue was akin to an outlaw motorcycle hangout crossed with a blind pig after-hours strip joint. Truth be told, my scout partner and I rarely ventured inside. We were content snagging drunk drivers leaving the club.

Dale Brown reminded me of a special forces' tac. officer at first glance; or had SWAT taken down the club? No, he wasn't SWAT;

1

Dale had a much harder job ... he was the peacekeeper in a lawless club.

As Dale approached our patrol car, it became clear that he wasn't the "police". Many police officers are territorial creatures, and they once looked upon Dale and his VIPERS as vigilantes or "wanna-bes." My curiosity was sparked. It was apparent that Dale wasn't a wannabe; he was the real thing — a protector! Dale greeted my part-ner and me with a smile and that now iconic eyebrow raised. That night would change my career and challenge my philosophy. It wasn't until several years later that Dale and I would join forces, and I learned Commander Brown's internal motivation.

At the turn of the century, I became a police community liaison trooper. Still curious about the man behind the eyebrow, I began training in Dale's Preventive Threat Management's exclusive and proprietary law enforcement defensive tactics system, the N.I.C.E. program (Non-Injury Compliance and Extraction). Ironically, after two decades, many of those police officers that looked upon Dale with disdain have been trained in the N.I.C.E. program. Dale was a practitioner and a student, and he also helped me with my State Po-lice efforts in the community.

For 17 years, we have partnered in more than 300 safety presenta-tions, including personal protection, active shooter response, work-place violence, and robbery awareness. We addressed sorority sisters to corporate CEOs and Fortune 500 corporations. I have heard many of the stories contained within this book during our presen-tations. As Dale gave these inspiring talks to the crowd, their dedi-cation to safety and protection won over the hearts of many.

I was privileged to witness the aftermath of many of his "victories "— a term given to domestic violence victims that Dale and his VIPERS assisted. These women, often with their children, not only received professional escorts, usually reserved for the elite of business executives, but were also empowered with Dale's urban survival tactics. Tactics that don't rely on prior fighting experience, strength, or gender. Many of the victors never returned to their tormentors and lived lives of peace and prosperity.

Dale's training benefited me as a law enforcement professional. I've used his N.I.C.E. tactics on the streets. During our department-sponsored defensive tactics training sessions, he dazzled my fellow troopers with his cutting-edge maneuvers.

My most valuable experience with Dale's training happened on the streets of downtown Detroit.

While on duty, I was flagged down by several city municipal workers.

They were frustrated with a homeless man who refused to vacate the grassy boulevard, preventing them from landscaping. The middle-aged homeless man was guarding his life possessions contained in a sack. When I got out of my patrol car, the homeless man pointed a knife at me and told me to "back off."

Because a knife was interjected into the scenario, some may have chosen to utilize deadly force. The incident could have been deemed "a good shooting" with little articulation. There is nothing ever good about taking a human life, particularly that of a vulnerable member of society with mental and emotional issues.

Immediately, I mirrored the man's intensity, lateraled to his side, thus physically and psychologically joining sides with him against the city workers. Before long, the homeless man put away the knife and placed his life's possessions in the trunk of my patrol vehicle. We met a block away, where I returned his belongings. Because of

Dale's training, mainly his tactical psychological component, I was able to preserve my life. When I first met Dale, I was an enforcer. Through his training, I changed into a community partner and then into a protector.

The engaging stories that you are embarking upon are more than the heroic feats of Dale Brown. They are stories of true love. Dale's love of humanity, Dale's love of people.

It's been said, "You cannot protect that which you do not love, and you cannot kill that which you love."

PREFACE

The Origin of D.T.M.C. and D.U.S.T.

The evolution of myself and my organization started when a girl was stripped and chased off a bridge in front of a crowd of people. Her name was Deletha Word. That year, 1995, I went from having a business model for protection services to creating a self-defense school that would teach people to defend themselves and to do it legally.

I was so outraged that day that I turned it into my life's purpose. I was no longer about making money and running a business; I was meant to help people learn how to defend themselves.

I cared more about training people on the east side of Detroit, locally known as "crack alley," where at-risk families by the hundreds are left unprotected. Vulnerable.

I opened the school there for everyone, shared self-defense tactics at what they could afford, and if they couldn't afford it at all, I would still train them.

My training systems grew over time, but starting out, they were mixed—those included knives, rifles, and fighting with legal structures.

I loved teaching families.

Then another turning point happened; a younger girl got attacked in front of me and I was attacked. I was threatened in front of my school, the school I had just opened, by gangs that were pointing guns.

The final straw was that I sought to be a community liaison, which turned into an organization.

When I stopped being a liaison, I then started being hired by the community.

I became an agent of change.

Twenty-seven years later, with no days off, we continue to be funded by sweat equity, self-funded, with no business loans, no government funds, or donations unless under special circumstances. And will continue to provide free, no-cost protection to anyone in need of protection from high-threat conditions in low-income and same-community areas as well as surrounding and rural areas.

The stories you will read will reflect the time between 1995 and 2012, real-life moments of encounter with DUST, and the application of tactics used in real-life scenarios.

-   Commander Dale C. Brown

INTRODUCTION

"I am an elite trooper—a sky trooper—a spearhead trooper." -Airborne Creed

---

1,250 Feet

Fort Benning, Georgia

Airborne School

August, 1989

Approximately 3:00 AM

A fire alarm blared.

My head shot up off the pillow. One of the other airborne school students had tripped the alarm. Awareness of my surroundings sunk in, the adrenaline subsided, and a sharp pain coursed through my neck.

It was the morning of the first jump, and I couldn't get my helmet on. A knot bulged from my neck, and my head was stuck at a tilt. I tried to correct it. There was a feeling like a knife entering between the vertebrae. The drill sergeants, known as black hats, wouldn't allow anyone to jump without a helmet.

Morning rise was at 5:00 AM. I walked outside, around 4:00, to a payphone. I called my mother. *Dr. Gale Northcross, US Army captain, a physician and was the most feared Army doctor I knew of.* I explained my injury.

"I don't think I can jump."

"You're just looking for a reason to fail." She replied.

"No, I'm not. I can't get my helmet on."

"Yes, you are."

"No, I'm not."

"Prove it."

The memory of Lieutenant Colonel Poteet flashed in his mind. Poteet was my JROTC instructor in high school in Ansbach, Germany. Poteet, from Alabama, resembled Colonel Sanders in military uniform.

"See this? Do you know what that is?" He barked.

"A skinhead with no neck?" I replied.

"This is what you"ll never be."

He was referring to the photograph of him mid-air, in full uniform as a paratrooper.

Unfazed, I responded, "Why would I jump out of a perfectly good aircraft? That's just dumb."

Two years after graduating high school, realizing I had no college options, I, Dale Brown, martial artist, survival expert, injured, and afraid of heights, was about to lose the opportunity to jump out of such an aircraft and prove everyone but myself right.

I decided to push forward. I got the helmet on with the chin strap hanging loose.

The group in training, known as non-airborne personnel (NAPs) or "dirty nasty legs," as the black hats liked to say, marched five agonizing miles in the summer heat of Georgia to a hanger. I lined up with the other NAPs.

One of the commanding officers noticed my tilted helmet in the crowd. "What's wrong with your head!" He yelled.

"Nothing, sir." I replied.

"Are you injured?"

"No, sir."

"Then you will put your head at an upright position and secure your chin strap."

I grimaced and grunted as the pain coursed up and down my spine. The black hat grabbed both sides of my head and tugged it into an upright position. Tears streamed down my face as my head quaked.

The strap snapped into place.

"If I see you with your strap unsecured again, I will drop you. Do you understand?"

"Yes, sir."

The C130 was the aircraft paratroopers typically deployed from.

What I saw was the largest, most intimidating aircraft that existed in the military, the C141. The craft looked big enough for a train to fit inside.. These planes were used primarily to transport tanks and other heavy loads of equipment. I remembered the past instruction: *"Never jump from a C141, or you will burn to death! Exiting the blast shield will cause your parachute to burn through you."*

I stood in line with about 200 other NAPs to board the ramp of the idling aircraft. I felt my heartrate spike. The pain in my neck spread to my chest. I became short of breath and began hyperventilating. I wondered if I was experiencing my first panic attack. As I surveyed the other troopers, I saw their lips and faces desperate for air like my own.

A C141 has four gigantic TF33 turbofan engines on each wing. These depleted the entire area of oxygen for the length of a football field. The only place to breathe was inside the aircraft.

The interior of the C141 was imposing. Unlike a commercial air-liner, it resembled the steel hold of a battleship. There were four rows of inward-facing seats. Every trooper was packed in tight, face to face, for as far as I could see. I recalled the airborne creed, "I am an elite trooper - a sky trooper - a spearhead trooper." It occurred to me that I was to be a part of the military songs sung about death from above and righteous violence. At that moment, I realized I was a member of an imperial invasion, much like the Roman Legion shock troopers. I was a cog in a larger-than-life force that both ter-rified and exhilarated me.

Once I boarded, one of the other cadets jumped from one seat to the next. I realized my assigned seat had just been taken. The seat left open was closest to the door and meant for the first man out.

Inside the craft, it was too loud to hear anyone speak. I used signals to share that my seat had been taken.

The jumpmaster, who looked something like Tom Cruise and wearing aviator sunglasses, approached me.

He yelled into my ear, "You will sit down, and you will stand up and walk out when I tell you to."

I sat, with my chinstrap still secure.

Most deployment flights, during training, are between 15 to 20 minutes. However, for re-certification, air force pilots must complete what is known as a 'contour flight.' To pass, the plane must be kept just above tree-level for 45 minutes. At the time, I didn't know what a contour flight was.

The plane took off.

An explosion of light rocked the pressurized cargo hold. My ears popped. The aircraft pitched as I felt I was going to be sucked out of the plane.

The jumpmaster gave the order, "Stand up!"

I repeated, "Stand up!" stood, and echoed the subsequent calls.

"Hook up!"

"Six minutes!"

"One minute!"

"Walk out!"

The order was directed at me. On the floor were flashing arrows pointing toward the open door and the words 'Walk Out.'

I walked to the opening. I felt the jumpmaster nudge me forward, more and more until the edge of his boots were no longer inside the aircraft.

The flight was turbulent, deafening, and violent. There was nothing to hold on to for stability. Instead, I gripped the spare chute attached to my abdomen, as instructed.

The jumpmaster, who I assumed was keeping me from falling out, but couldn't feel anything, repeatedly yelled in my ear.

"When I tap your shoulder, you will walk out, do you understand?"
"Yes, sir!"

For the next 45 minutes, I stood, the toe of his boot hanging over open sky, as they flew at 1,250 feet above the ground. The trees appeared close enough to touch until he felt a tap upon his shoulder and heard the order.

I walked out.

My primary parachute was to release from a static line automatically.

For mass deployment, paratroopers are dropped at a low altitude between 1,250 and 8000 feet. High altitude, low open (HALO) drops were considered much safer. The logic of low-altitude drops is that the soldier will be shot at by enemy combatants once the parachute is deployed. Once a trooper exits the aircraft, he is instructed to count: one thousand, two thousand, three thousand, four thousand. At four seconds, if the primary chute hasn't opened, the paratrooper is to release the D-rings, turn his head to the left, and feed the spare up past his face to avoid 'bounce' or landing without a parachute.

I was in free fall and screaming. My body was in a tight tuck position like a professional diver, in an L-shape.

I inverted and saw the aircraft over my feet, flying away, as the chute opened.

The powerful thrumming of the aircraft was gone. There was no wind rushing. All was suddenly silent, peaceful. An intense high overtook me.

Dale Brown, that day, at that moment, was reborn into a world without limitations.

The screaming of 100s of troopers, male and female, filled the air.

1

The Belle Isle Bridge

Detroit, Michigan

August 1995

A young mother and daughter leave their dog behind as they run for their lives. Three large young men, the size of football players, follow closely behind. The mother and child get into their car and sped towards the bridge that connects Belle Isle to greater Detroit.

This is a weekend, so the bridge is packed. The woman's car slowed to a stop behind a row of red taillights.

The young men rush between the idling vehicles. The leader has a crowbar. They find the car and wedge the door open. The woman is pulled out as she screamed from the driver's seat.

As this is going on, approximately 30 people exit their vehicles and formed a crowd. Everyone stands by as if watching a spectator sport while the young men rip her clothes off. Loud cheering is heard.

During the struggle, the young mother breaks free. She bolts, half naked and screaming, while the men resume chasing her. They gain on her. Realizing she has nowhere else to run to, she turn and jump off the bridge into the rushing water below.

Two young observers, weighing approximately 150 to 180 pounds each, dive off the bridge after her. They hit the water and resurfaced a moment later. The young mother does not.

****

I came to Detroit to teach self-defense because of the mother's story on the Belle Isle bridge. It revealed an important reason for my existence and my training system. I was a lifeguard, a swim instructor and taught self-defense at the Y.M.C.A. in 1994. I knew that she would still be alive if I had been on that bridge or trained a student.

The story broke the day it happened and was put on high rotation on CNN for a week and recounted through interviews worldwide. The city of Detroit experienced global humiliation.

The backstory is that of a young football player who wouldn't take "no" for an answer. He'd gone to private schools, was articulate and intelligent, and held a football scholarship to the University of Michigan.

The young lady was gorgeous and approximately 33 years old. She was on Belle Isle, the biggest island connected to any city in the U.S.A. It's about one mile long and six miles in circumference. The island is famous as a party place for young people and an adult vacation spot. The woman was walking her dog by the river when the men began hitting on her. She was so scared that she left her dog behind when she fled.

The water runs about 30 feet below the bridge, which spans four lanes across. The day after the woman died, I stood on the bridge. Even though I had been an airborne paratrooper, a lifeguard, and a swim instructor and had done extensive research on where to jump off, I never found a place I felt comfortable enough to actually do it. I wanted to jump, get it on camera, and show it could be done. I never did. It is terrifying. The water is 30–40 feet deep. The current is fast and strong. Steel, cars, debris, and dead bodies can be found below the surface. The two men who jumped in to save the woman did so without hesitation, but they couldn't see anything in the dark water. The undertow is very powerful and is known for dragging people from the shallow areas around the island.

When I first heard the story, I didn't believe it was true. I was sure the media was lying. There's no way a crowd of people would jump and cheer while something like that was happening. Later, I found out that's what groups tend to do. That is how a group dynamic works. Random people who don't know the victim or the attacker will root and cheer for the attacker. No one steps up because they assume someone else will.

The internet wasn't a thing in 1995. I thought the news lied. Years later, I found online testimonials of people who were on the bridge that day. It was true. It happened.

The young men who jumped off the bridge received an award on Channel 4. I was very proud of them. I remember thinking, "Wow, these are some real heroes. I can't imagine jumping off that bridge.'

Chapter 1 Lessons

- Some men can't take "no" for an answer.
- ~~Group settings are safe.~~
- With our training, those two heroes could have avoided jumping off the bridge after Ms. Ward by jumping in before the attackers chased her off the bridge.

2

Method Man: First Encounter

Detroit, Michigan

East Jefferson Avenue

1995

Approximately 4:00 PM

The sound of gunfire ricochets off the high-rises on the east side of Detroit. I can hear it clearly from my apartment. It sounds like it's right outside my window. No more than 100 yards away, there is an individual firing in broad daylight.

The Boulevard, East Jefferson, is a busy one and the largest in Detroit. It spans six lanes across, running from downtown into the wealthy suburbs of Grosse Pointe. Approximately 10 apartment buildings along the corridor were built in the 1920s and 1940s: once beautiful art decor in run-down conditions. The mayor's mansion rests in an eyeshot of the scene. The Jeffersonian, a prominent residential building for judges, law enforcement, and politicians, sits on the same block.

Every day, at 4:00 PM, I hear the gun going off. It's very disruptive to myself and the surrounding families. I call the police like I have been every day around this time for the last four months. All of the 911 operators know me by name. They know I'm calling about the gunshots.

"Dale, is this Dale? You're calling about the shooting, right? We're sending someone."

I'm security for the building I live in. I'm tired of hearing what sounds like a gunfight in my front yard. Bullets are flying over 100s of cars and drivers. *What are the people in those cars thinking and feeling?*

I grab my rifle: a modified SKS 7.62 by 39 millimeter with a folding block stock, a 30-round magazine bipod, supported muzzle brake, and scope with the illuminated red and green reticule. The site includes a four and mounted pressure switch laser and flashlight.

I move to the balcony atop a liquor store. I can see the individual; an African American male, approximately six feet, 250 pounds. He's firing hollow-point black rounds at a STOP Sign from a .45 caliber Smith & Wesson semi-automatic pistol. He takes notice of me elevated 50 feet behind him.

I adopt a shooting position. I keep the barrel of the rifle pointed downward at a 45-degree angle.

The shooter has a buddy with him. The gunman turns to me and yells, "My man can't shoot! Shoot the STOP Sign!"

"What?" I reply.

"Shoot the STOP Sign! My man here can't shoot."

"I can only shoot shooters."

He balks. "What?"

"I said I can only shoot *shooters!*" My voice booms in a deep low tone.

At that, he stops shooting. I watch them cross the street and enter an apartment building.

Two police officers arrive. After a quick recap of events, I lead them into the gunman's building. We find him hanging out in the hall. He's stashed the gun somewhere off his person. There's no search warrant. The police officers question him and poke around a bit. He tells them he lives there. They realize there's not much they can do. The officers leave.

Unsatisfied by how easily this individual is getting off, I approach. I notice a striking resemblance to the rapper Method Man.

I ease in close. "Look, man, I'm going to tell you how it is. Tomorrow, you can't be here. You've got 24 hours. I'm not discussing it. You just can't be here."

"Whatever, man." He says and goes into one of the units.

****

I had to learn these lessons the hard way. My worldviews were challenged, often wholly destroyed, and redefined to suit a reality wherein I could be effective.

The particular situation illustrated above marks the beginning of a critical transitional period in my life. I was 25 years old. I had moved to the east side of Detroit with little more than a pit bull mix puppy and my modified SKS. The area seemed like a nicer one by comparison before I moved in. I quickly discovered that was not the case.

I had been a soldier, never a police officer, and was becoming a proactive agent of change.

Later, I learned that 4:00 PM was the optimum time for this individual to use a busy boulevard as his shooting range. He was sending a message, as criminals like to do. He knew when shift change for the police was. Forty-five minutes before and 45 minutes after 4:00 PM, the police weren't available to respond to 911 calls in person.

I also learned that taking a strategically advantageous position with superior firepower worked to de-escalate the situation without violence. Keeping my gun at a 45-degree angle, while not entirely non-threatening, was not pointed at him. A more directly threatening posture could have provoked a shootout. I had ended the shooting without having to fire a shot.

Chapter 2 Lessons

- Position yourself strategically for the perceived threat.
- Use superior firepower.
- Keep your firearm drawn downward at a 45-degree angle when approaching a threat.

Throughout this book, I share essential lessons in psychology, tactics, and what I have coined, Threat Management. That includes, to a large extent, lessons in which I unlearned what I thought I knew.

3

Crack Alley

Detroit, Michigan

East Jefferson Avenue

October 31, 1995

Approximately 4:00 PM

It's Halloween. Every year in Detroit, the day before, of, and after Halloween, I can expect to hear guns going off day and night. Full automatic gunfire sounds throughout the streets of "Crack Alley," which is the area encompassing the streets of East Jefferson, Hibbard, Agnes, and Holcomb. It sounds like a revolution.

Bullets come down. They hit people; they kill people. *Families are losing family members, and for what?* I hear a particular assault rifle firing more than usual. Typically, the shooter goes through one magazine per day. On Halloween, it's in complete celebration; firing, reloading, firing, reloading, all day. I call the police again and again. I tell them this guy is blasting nonstop, but it's not enough.

I rigged a spotlight on top of my white Bronco II. My logo and the words "Survival Instructor" show on the side of my vehicle. I hop in with my rifle and head towards Precinct 5, the police station.

They tell me I'm at the wrong precinct and need to go to Precinct 7. I find Precinct 7 and report the shooting again. The front desk tells me I need to call the police. I explain that I already have.

"Well, go to the scene, call us, and we'll send someone."

"OK!" I replied.

I head back, wondering how I will find this guy—the distinct 30 rounds of gunfire echo through the neighborhood. The streets go quiet, and I wait. He reloads, and the firing restarts. My Bronco moves closer. I'm pinning this guy down, one full magazine at a time, hoping he'll keep it up.

A muzzle flash appears in the window of one home. It's the gunman, and he's shooting into an abandoned house across the way. *Why is he doing this? What is the point?* I have no idea, and so far, there's no squad car. I never gave them an address, so they don't know the exact location.

While making rounds throughout the area, I spot a red or burgundy Crown Victoria. These are known as "cherries" or "cherry cars" parked nearby. I assume it's a specialized unit. I'm excited. Four officers sit inside wearing plaid shirts. They always wear plaid shirts; it's a thing. Three of them are asleep, and the one in the driver's seat is awake.

Politely, I approach and speak to the driver. "Hey, how's it going? You guys are here for the gunshots?"

"What?" the driver responds.

"The guy shooting, you guys are here for that?"

Full automatic fire sounds throughout the neighborhood again.

"That! Right there, right there!"

He looks at me, "Umm, well, why don't you show us where this is coming from."

The Bronco fires up. I head back to the house with the cherry car following close behind. I pull up and shine my spotlight directly onto the house. The shooter knows the cavalry has arrived. The cherry blows past me and pulls over to the curb, roughly 150 yards away.

I can't see the shooter. I don't hear any gunfire. I turn the light off and slowly back out. My Bronco pulls up next to the cherry car, and I exit the vehicle. The driver is a police sergeant. He's scanning my vehicle.

"Umm, Mr. Brown. It says here you are a survival instructor, is that correct?" He asked.

"Yes, Sir. That's correct." I answered.

"Well, let me ask you this. Does it sound very survival-oriented to pull up to a gunman's house and point a light on it? Does that sound very survival-*ish* to you?"

"Umm, no."

"Yeah, I didn't think so. We're going to put the information in the system. A detective will get back to you. But what were you thinking?"

"Honestly, just so we're clear. My survival training isn't for me. It's meant for others. My survival is secondary to the people I protect." I replied.

"Oh, OK."

"I protect people. But I see where you're coming from."

"Whatever."

The cherry car leaves the scene, and so do I.

****

Crack Alley isn't what you'd expect at first glance. It contains 10 apartment buildings, and 400 dwellings, about 10 percent of which are criminals, and the remaining 90 percent are families.

Subdivisions like Crack Alley give Detroit its reputation as a hotbed for criminal activity, including murder, robbery, and rape. My frustration grew as a direct result of misunderstanding law enforcement procedures. Gunfire from a fully automatic rifle is loud, terrifying, and disruptive. The surrounding families were being terrorized by an individual I met later on. He was a drug dealer firing his rifle daily to establish dominance in the neighborhood. In essence, he was marking his territory.

Even in Detroit, where calls come in nonstop, crime has crippled the city's economy. Law enforcement does not imply police officers actively seeking trouble or rooting out criminals. Cops are people. They're eager to get home to their lives and families every day, just like you. The conversation with the sergeant left me deflated, but not without having learned a couple of valuable lessons.

Chapter 3 Lessons

- I realized my mission was fundamentally different.

4

Method Man:

Second Encounter**

Detroit, Michigan

East Jefferson Avenue

November 1995

Approximately 2:00 PM

The phone rings, and I hear a frantic lady on the line.

"Help me! Help me! This guy just robbed me with five guys! They took the only thing I own, which is one dresser! They made me take my kids' clothes out and give them the dresser. He said he was going to knock the door down if I don't just give him the dresser!"

"What?" I replied.

"Yeah, it was that guy who always shoots in front of the building."

"What!"

"Yeah!"

She's been dealing with what I call thug animals for too long. I talk her into calling the cops. After making the call, I head to the victim's apartment.

I enter her home. Her kids' clothes are scattered on the floor.

The first thing she says is, "The police aren't going to do anything."

"They will. They will do something. You just have to know how to explain everything, and they will do their job." I replied.

"No, they *won't.*

Two officers show up. I approach.

"Officers, she is the victim, right here. They took her stuff, strong-armed robbed her, and she'll be a witness. The guys who did this are down the street. I already know what apartment they're in."

One officer responds, "Where is this?"

"It's right down the street." I replied.

The officers follow my white Bronco II, we pull up to the building, and I jump out with my rifle.

The two officers yell, "Hey! You can't do that! You can't have a rifle out here!"

I freeze and attempt to make sense of what they're saying. "Yes, you can. This is an open-carry state. Plus, I'm security for the building, so it wouldn't matter either way."

"Well, we're not going in there." The cops respond.

"You don't have to. I'll bring him out to you. Please stand by."

I enter the building and rush up to the top floor. I know who this guy hangs out with. I go to the door and tell him to come out.

The door cracks open, and I see what I can only describe as a crack-head looking at me through the door jam. His eyes bulge as he peeks out.

"Where's the guy?" I say.

His head shakes, "I dunno', I dunno."

"Listen to me. I'm only going to tell you this once—you know what— he's standing right there, isn't he?

He has a gun and is prepared to shoot through the door. I can see he's scanning my rifle barrel that's leveled directly at him. I have 30 rounds of steel core ammunition, an extended magazine, a bipod, and a large muzzle brake.

He's clearly impressed. My ammunition is much more powerful than his own.

I give the order again. "Just come out. If you start shooting, you will get shot."

He turns and starts yelling, "Get out! get out!"

Method Man walks out with his hands in the air. I cuff him and walk him out of the building. We make it outside. The police are gone.

"Alright, let me go now." He says.

"Man, I'm not letting you go *nowhere*. Ever. Think about what you did. You went to a single mom's house with three children and *robbed* her. You're going to jail. That's where you're going."

"Man, this some bullsh*t."

"Listen, you're shooting a gun at people. You could kill people. I tell you that you can't just leave. Why would you rob this lady? She has nothing! She only had one thing. Why would you steal that from her and her children?"

He responds. "Man, 'cuz you told me I only had one day left. So I had to go. I had to take somethin'. You know what I'm sayin'?"

"That's the logic you're using? Because you were told you can't shoot your gun at people, around people, and terrorize people; you rob them? So, you can leave?"

"Man, whatever man, I needed money. I had to do what I had to do."

"OK, well, you made the wrong decision. Now you must sit down and wait for the police. It's going to be a minute."

Method Man sits next to me with his hands cuffed behind his back. I'm calling the police repeatedly.

Three hours go by. At this point, we are sharing life stories.

"You know you look like—"

"I know, I get that all the time." He says.

"You do; you really look just like Method Man."

"Man, I can't feel my arms. I been sittin' here for three hours."

He goes on, "Man, just let me go."

I'm getting worried about his arms. I half-want his autograph. No good options are apparent.

Reluctantly I say, "OK, look, Method Man. I'm going to let you go since I came to the realization that the police aren't showing up. But you have to *promise* never to come back around here."

"I promise. I promise. I won't come back." He replied.

"You promise!"

"I *promise*, man. I'll just go away, and I won't come back."

A police cruiser pulls in front of us. I speak to the driver, "How's it going, officers?" I asked.

"What's going on here?" The officer replied.

"You guys were sent to pick up the guy for home invasions?"

"No, I don't know what you're talking about. Is that your white Bronco parked over there?"

I see that I parked it funny. I explain the situation and that I've been calling for the past three hours.

Method Man protests. "Man, you said I could go, man!"

"Yeah. Sorry about that. Not really, though. Don't rob single moms with three children. It's just not good."

The officers put him in the back of the squad car and leave.

****

The woman in the story is one that I meet again on a later day. At this stage, I couldn't comprehend the reason behind police actions. I didn't understand how criminals made decisions. Here we have a single mom, who I discovered worked three jobs and has three kids. The only thing she owned of any value was a huge dresser. It was a nice piece that five grown men had decided to take, with the threat of violence, and carried away down the street.

I had the so-called Method Man dead to rights. I had him for a home invasion with a witness and the victim. In Michigan, that crime will put you away for 20 years. On top of that, I had him for possession of the stolen property, and he had a gun. He was looking at 30 years or more in prison.

At this point in my evolution, I was young and naive.

Chapter 4 Lessons

- Show of superior force (my rifle, ammunition, scope, etc.) is a powerful motivator to prevent a violent outcome.
- Criminals prioritize profiting.

5

Taxicab Shuffle

Detroit Michigan

Hibbard Street

August 1995

Between 1:00 AM and 6:00 AM*

Beautiful Gothic architecture lines Hibbard Street. The apartment buildings were built in the 1920s and 1940s. Massive pillars grace the apartment buildings in what resembles Gotham City. The skyline juts and dips. The building heights range from three to 17 stories. Each building contains between 50 and 100 units, and no one is sleeping tonight.

I'm at my post behind the Hibbard Apartments building and wondering what to make of the sprawling scene in front of me. It's the Grand Central Station of Taxicabs. An endless row of cabs floods the street. It's beyond noisy. Doors are opening and slamming. Men are conversing and making deals as if this was the heart of Downtown on a Friday Night. This goes on all night and has been for the past few days.

The surrounding families are upset; there's no peace for the families here with this level of racket. They feel powerless to do anything. However, tonight, I'm prepared for the Taxicab shuffle.

I see little more than male silhouettes. It's too dark to discern faces, and I'm far away. Ahead of me, from an elevated guard tower, a light shines down on the cabs. The source comes from a spotlight that I attached to a tripod-mounted camera. The catch is I can't afford recording hardware. It's a dummy camera, *but they don't know that.*

The cabs start backing out. Their licenses, displayed on the back plates, are at stake. They're doing something illegal, and they believe I know what that is. A few cabs take a different route to avoid the camera.

The next day, I position the camera more aggressively. If a cab comes down this part of Hibbard street, they will see there's no escaping the all-seeing dysfunctional camera.

More cabs back out. The streets are emptying. Within a few days, the neighborhood regains its peaceful ambiance. I know families are sleeping soundly again, and I'm pretty damn proud of myself.

Daylight hits, and I'm in the guard tower. A female approaches. She's in shape, attractive, wearing plain clothes, and approximately 25 years of age.

As I am looking down at her from the guard tower, she turns toward me and says, "Why are you doing that?"

She's articulate. I assume she's a college student, but I have no clue what she's referring to.

"Doing what?" I replied.

"You're stopping our customers! We can't get our customers because the cabs won't bring our people!"

It dawns on me that this woman is a prostitute, referring to the Taxi traffic on Hibbard. I had broken up a prostitution ring in the neighborhood without knowing it.

I attempt to keep things cordial, not make any personal attacks, and focus on the real issue. "Ma'am, we can't have these engines. I live right there. The engines are too loud."

She's irate. "You're ruining our business. It's how we pay our bills!"

"I'm not trying to tell you how to make your money. We can't have traffic that interferes with the quality of life of the families in the community. You are preventing children from being able to sleep at night as a result of vehicles and traffic in and out of the buildings. I'm not passing any kind of judgment on your profession. We can't have the traffic which is disturbing the families."

She cusses me out.

****

This story marks where I learned that there is a non-violent way to make a significant impact and cause immediate change. Had I politely asked the Taxi drivers to be considerate, threatened a neighborhood uprising, or even threatened to call the police, the cab drivers would not have been concerned. It amazed me how the fear of being recorded caused such a reaction.

The cabs dropped off the johns, the johns dropped their pants and cash, hopped back in the cabs, and rolled out. They had a system, and they were there to make a buck. But the threat of losing a steady income stream was enough to alter their behavior entirely. Now, had they been caught aiding illegal activity, they would have lost their licenses and been fined up to 10,000 dollars.

The quality of life of stakeholders in the community matters. It requires the sacrifices of people within the community that infringes upon the liberty and happiness of others. In this case, that sacrifice was the neighborhood prostitutes. While I still ended up being cussed out, I had made a point not to point fingers of any kind at the young woman approaching me in the tower. I was concerned with the cars and traffic. I kept a focus on the community, not morals or the laws.

Chapter 5 Lessons

- Non-violent action works.
- Focus on achievable objectives, not ideal ones.
- Communities lack services that provide community-focused protection.

6

Hi Dummy

Detroit, Michigan

Hibbard and East Jefferson

Late November 1995

Approximately 10:00 PM

The floor of the guard tower hovers ten feet from the ground. The construction consists mostly of wood, steel inside, and ten by five bulletproof glass. The building owner had crafted it himself. Inside is my staged video camera mounted on a tripod. Next to it stands my sidekick, a makeshift dummy I threw together using a wet suit, a leather jacket, and a motorcycle helmet. The camera doesn't record, but the spotlight works, and it shines out on the lot.

A parking lot sprawls out before the tower with some 100 cars parked in it. I watch through the scope of my rifle from 50 yards back. I notice a Monte-Carlo parking in the distance. The paint job is custom, dark and looks sinister in a sophisticated car-show kind of way.

Two men walk away from the car towards the tower. They're African American, around six-foot each, medium builds, one bald, the other with long braids, and 25 to 30 years old. Their clothes are urban fashionable with brightly colored leather jackets. They unknowingly pass by me, about 20 feet away, at a relaxed gait. They're clean-cut. I assume they're going to a party. However, I don't like how the car is parked.

They approach the guard tower, smile at the camera, wave, and keep walking until they're out of sight.

OK?

Ten minutes pass, and I see them stalk up to the tower again. They wave again. After that, they return to the strangely parked car, hop in, and book it out of the parking lot.

Weird.

Then a man randomly comes running up to my post. I begin to recognize him. He's European-American, about 6'5, 350 pounds wearing a dirty t-shirt and dirty shorts. He looks like an alcoholic or maybe a drug-abuser. He's around 30 years of age. He is the husband of the assistant manager for the building I'm tasked with protecting.

"Did you see those guys? Did you see those guys? They just robbed me! They just robbed me!" He yells.

I try to respond, but I'm dumbfounded.

****

The two individuals remained entirely calm for and from the robbery. They looked into the camera, thinking I was a dummy, and assuming the camera worked. They didn't wear masks. They took no measures to hide their identity. The dysfunctional camera did absolutely nothing in terms of stopping this crime. I am amazed by the audacity of these two guys.

A predator's mindset is very different from that of an ordinary person. Patterns of behavior often appear bizarre and rarely show signs of panic or apprehension. Unlike the Taxi drivers, who reacted with fear to my camera, these were real violent criminals who did not perceive my camera as the slightest concern. While that may seem like a miscalculation on their part, the truth is that I didn't understand something fundamental. When criminals believe you are incapable of negatively affecting them, they don't care about you or your camera. There must be more than just the idea you will tell them when dealing with violent predators. They do not fear you because they don't respect you when they think you're incapable of stopping them. They knew there wouldn't be any investigation or substance that would allow them to be taken into custody.

A camera can help you in terms of preserving your safety. However, it is only one component of your protection, not a panacea. It can prevent escalation but often does not prevent predation. To effectively deter violent criminal behavior, you must instill the belief that there is no need for violence, no gain from violence, and no chance of successful violence.

Chapter 6 Lessons

- Real predators rarely behave as expected.
- Criminals often park strategically in obscure places before committing a crime.
- ~~Dangerous criminals fear cameras.~~

7

The Big Dog Puppy

Detroit, Michigan

Corner of Hibbard and East Jefferson

Late August 1995

Midday

It's broad daylight, and I'm standing at the corner of East Jefferson Avenue and Hibbard Street. A woman screams. I see the woman, a hard-working professional, exit the driver side of the Taxicab. She's small-statured, middle-aged, with pale skin and gray-blondish hair. She's slightly disheveled, and I can hear the hint of a Boston accent as she yells, "Help me! Help me! He tried to carjack me! He tried to attack me!"

I see a large African-American male walking away from the Taxi. He's big, 6'4", roughly 300 pounds, and 35 to 40 years old. I immediately name him "Green Mile" in my mind. I take off in his direction.

At my side is my puppy. The dog's a pit bull German Shepard mix, about six months old and only 20 pounds. He's not very big but

45

looks hardcore enough, like a young brindle Mastiff.

I follow after Green Mile. He rounds the corner, heading West on East Jefferson. His gait picks up; he must have noticed me. I take off into a run, and he speeds up in turn. I circle in front of him in a McDonald's parking lot near the corner of Hibbard.

"I didn't do nothin'!" Green Mile has a heavy lisp. He sounds like Mike Tyson, only slower.

"Sit down!" I yell.

My dog is very excited. He's wiggling around and crying while I hold it by the harness. The dog is not vicious. I can tell it wants to play and possibly cuddle with Green Mile, nothing more. He's eyeing the dog intensely. He's terrified. I can tell he's thinking of making a run for it.

"Sit down and wait for the Police!" I repeat, "Don't make me let this dog go!"

"OK! OK!"

Green Mile sits on the ground. The dog's still wiggling. I call the police; they show up and take him away without incident.

***

I learned later that the man had a mental condition. He was off his meds. His surprising fear of the dog and his childlike manner of speech tipped me off. It would have been inappropriate to have had to use violence on an individual in his state. The dog, as young as it was, worked as a show of force. That day I learned how powerful people's fear of animals could be. The perception of superior strength, not the power itself, motivates submissive behavior. No violence was necessary.

Chapter 7 Lessons

- Dogs work well as a show of force.
- To create compliance, there must be a trust bond established. In other words, the subject must believe that compliance will result in no injury to prevent resistance to subjugation.
- The criminal, in this situation, believed that compliance was the best way to avoid violence, and he was right.

8

Security Daze

Detroit, Michigan

The Hibbard Apartments

Early September 1995

Midday

The owner of the Hibbard Apartment Building hired me as security. We cut a deal. I would work for $4.50 an hour, billed for 40 hours a week. The minimum wage at this point is 5.15, but I'm happy.

In front of the Hibbard Apartment Building, I hear a disturbance. Three stories up, from one of the windows, are two men with rifles yelling.

"Die! Die!"

They're cocking and clicking their rifles. As far as I can tell, they're dry firing. No bullets are flying.

A man is crossing the lawn to his car. I yell for him to go back into the building, and he takes off.

I take cover behind a steel garbage can. I have no idea what's going on. I can't tell if they're shooting at us or acting like fools. The modified SKS is on my back. I bring it forward and take aim. Through my scope, I see the men in the apartment building. Their weapons appear to be a sawed-off shotgun and an AK-47.

In 1995, very few people owned a cellular phone, except the FBI, El Chapo, and myself. I pull out my phone and call 911.

Within minutes, police cars screech up to the building. Thirty officers move into the building. I decide to put my gun away and return to the guard tower. The police are on high alert. Any gunman would appear as a threat. Friendly fire happens quite often under these circumstances.

I return to the building. Every one of the officers must be inside. I book it to the third floor, where the hall is full of officers lining the walls. They've found the unit with the gunmen, and we hear them through the door. They're racking and cocking their weapons in an acoustic show of threat.

One of the officers yells, "Come out!"

The gunmen respond, "You come through that door we gonna' blast yo a**!"

"If you don't open that door, I'm gonna' kick it in!" The cop yells back.

"I'm not openin' the door!"

I realize that this gigantic cop is not bluffing. I can hardly believe he's about to kick this door in, and I'm going to watch him die.

He kicks the door in and walks inside.

From the hallway, I hear the officer's voice. "Where's the guns at?"

"We don't have any guns! We don't have any guns!"

The officers in the hallway move in.

Three stories below, outside the building, Scorpio watches the guns fall to the ground. He's my first trainee. If Eminem had a little brother, he would look just like Scorpio. His weapon of choice is a large combat knife.

The officers and I realize the guns got tossed and are sitting in the grass outside the building. The gunmen are taken into custody.

The next day, I get a call from an old Jewish lady that lives in the building. She's in her 80s or 90s and hates my guts. I offered her security services in the past, and she told me to beat it, that she never wanted to see me again. This time, she's upset with me for bringing the police to her building for the men dry firing out the window. She's been in the building since the 1960s.

Over the phone, she says, "I need you to come over here to talk about something."

She sounds less mean this time. She must actually need help. Or she's mad and hiding it.

I head over to her apartment unit. The sound of construction blares throughout the building. It's so loud that I can hardly hear her inside the apartment.

"Ma'am, I'm sorry, can you speak up? I'm having trouble hearing you. What were you saying?"

She responds, "What do you charge for the month?"

"Oh, it's two hundred dollars for the month."

"Two hundred dollars? Done!" She cuts a check.

I pocket it feeling pretty proud of myself.

"Now, what I need you to do is get that guy out of my building."-
She says.

"What guy?" I asked.

"The guy you hear tearing up my building!"

"Isn't that construction?"

"No! He's on the third floor! He's knocking down the windows and
the doors! He's tearing out the pipes! I need help!"

"Did you call the police?"

"Yes, I did. I've been waiting for two hours. I donate money to
them every year. I've donated thousands of dollars to the police. I'm
very upset right now!"

I'm amazed that a single individual is responsible for causing all this
noise. It sounds like a construction crew hard at work.

"OK, let me go get my rifle."

"Hurry back!"

On my way out, on every floor, tables are destroyed. Doors and fire
doors are broken. Broken glass litters the halls.

It's put up or shut up time.

I get the rifle and return.

I locate the unit with the individual holed up inside. It's the same unit the officer kicked in. Half of the door is gone. A blanket covers the remaining aperture. I knock on what's left of the door.

I hear his voice. "I'm not gonna' tell you, whoever you are, get away from my door. I just got out of prison. I'm a killer. Wanna' know who I am? Call the FBI because I'm a killer! I kill people! Ima' kill! I kill cops, and I'm gonna' kill you if you knock on that door again."

I respond, "Sir, this is security. You have to leave the building immediately. You understand?"

"When I open this door, it's goin' down. I'm tellin' you now! When I open this door, don't say I didn't warn you! I told you to go to the FBI and find out who I am!"

I knock on the door with my extended muzzle brake.

"I warned you! I warned you!" He yanks the door open with a yell. The barrel of my rifle is now inches from his face.

His expression drops. He's breathing heavily and struggling to speak. "Wha-what's the AK for?"

"Move slowly. Gather your things. We're leaving now." I commanded.

"OK!"

He gathers a speaker full of clothing, and I walk him down the stairs and out of the building. He leaves. In three minutes, this guy is gone.

I return to the Jewish lady's unit to let her know he's gone.

She's surprised to see me. "You got him out that quickly?"

"Yes, ma'am."

"Wow, it was worth every dollar."

We hear screeching tires. I peek my head out the window. Below, the scene looks like something out of a movie. 30 officers appear heavily armed outside and stacked alongside the wall.

I walk out of the building towards the officers. I use my most official-sounding voice, "How's it going, gentleman? How are you?" My voice tone sounds funny to me, like a Fed in a crime movie.

The closest officer looks tense. He keeps his voice in a strained whisper. "We got a call about a man with a gun. A gunman. That threw a man out of an apartment with a gun."

"Oh yeah, that'd be me. This is my gun right here."

He looks perplexed. The other officers do, too. "What?"

"Yes, I'm security for the building. The guy with the dust between his braids and the prison identification on his wrist. That guy was trespassing and threatening to kill people and was in an apartment that was abandoned. He doesn't live here. He has no belongings here."

"Really?" He responds.

"Really." I repeat.

Later in the day, I teach my self-defense class. I have 15 kids and about ten adults. It's a very multicultural class. They're African-American, Bolivian, European-American, and mixed ethnicities. The front window of the flat looks out on Jefferson Avenue. On the walls, there are different weapons for training: shotguns, pistols, rifles, knives, batons, long-staffs, AR-15s, MP5s, and more. A life-size dummy for kicking and punching hangs out. I use a mattress with a plastic sheet as a landing pad for various activities.

The kids and adults are facing me. Behind them is the front door, which I keep open during the summer. Two men appear in the doorway. They don't look friendly. One is thin, about six feet, and the other is shorter and thicker. They begin to make noise.

"We C-down mother*cker! We C-down!" They form their hands into the letter C.

C-down?

"We C-down! You don't bring the po-lice to our house! We beat the case! Now what! Now what! We C-down."

I sigh. "First of all, I don't know what C-down means."

I turn toward the class. "Kids, this is what you do when people are violent and disruptive."

I walk towards the open doorway. The two men put up their hands, ready to fight. "Alright! C'mon! C'mon!"

I slam the door in their faces and turn the lock.

It's quiet for a beat, and then I hear, "We goin' to getcho' ass!"

****

The two men who disrupted my class and threatened me were the same two who tossed the guns and went into custody. They were put in jail for one day and beat the case. On the day they were dry firing, they were likely drunk, high, or both while menacing pass-ersby for entertainment.

It took a little time to put together what had transpired. Scorpio, my trainee, was the only witness to the guns being tossed out the window. However, his word wasn't official enough in the eyes of the law. The weapons had a tape, which worked against any fingerprinting that would indict the men.

The prosecutor was frustrated with the police because they hadn't followed protocol. If police officers surround a violent criminal that's taken up shelter, at least one officer must be left outside. Had just one officer seen the guns tossed from the building, the two men wouldn't have been set free.

I later learned that the individual destroying the Jewish lady's building was related to the two men. He was an ex-con and was out for revenge. Even though he was unarmed, he didn't expect much resistance by sheer intimidation alone. He hadn't expected anyone, fully armed, to stand up to him.

"C-down" indicates that the two men at my school were gang-affiliated as Crips. Having gotten out of jail, they were out for revenge. They did this by attacking my business. While I felt some victory from avoiding physical combat, they knew what they were doing. My students' parents were upset because my school wasn't a safe place for their children.

Chapter 8 Lessons

- Faith ineffective security can be restored, even for 80-year-old ladies
- Criminals retaliate

9

Raid

Part 1

Detroit, Michigan

East Jefferson Avenue

Brian, code name Bravo-1, and I work on tactics daily at my training center. When calls come in, we head out. And after that, we get back to the tactics. Most days that means training for 12 hours. It's easy to train all the time when you're broke.

A lady calls us. She's a local barber. Her voice is frantic, "Someone is shooting over here."

Bravo-1 and I arrive at 1130 Holcomb in full tactical gear. The words "U.S. Patrol" are stitched on our uniforms. A man with a shotgun hangs out in the front. We look like a para-military unit.

He's the assistant manager of the building. I suspect he's the one firing.

"Hey, what are you doing with that gun?"

He's relaxed. His voice holds no defensive tone. "Yeah, I was shooting the gun."

"What's the situation?" I asked.

"There's a carjacker who pistol-whipped an old man here." He responded.

The apartment building has about 50 units and a 15 by 15 foot vestibule. Four stories and roughly 50 percent occupancy. It's the same building that we pulled Method Man out of.

"Give me that shotgun."

He hands it over, and I unload it. Black number six shots for a 12 gauge shotgun. I count he's three shells shy, so I'm reasonably sure he's telling the truth about being the shooter.

"Next time, don't shoot. Just call us."

He nods.

I believe he's trying to help, so I respond, "You should leave."

He takes off.

Down the hall, I see three men. Bravo-1 and I approach. One looks about 80 years old. He's bleeding from the mouth. The other two are younger, athletic, and clean cut. One's wearing a jogging suit. I know he works as a janitor in the building. He's telling the other guy to back off.

The second younger male has his hand placed on his waistband. The jogging suit tells me the other is the carjacker and has a gun.

Fifteen feet down the hall, women, are screaming and yelling profanity. I count about 10, all women, ages 20 to 40. They're using a two-by-four as a battering ram.

The carjacker yells, "I'm going to kill you bit*h! Open the door bit*h!"

The screams of children can be heard from inside.

"Stop hitting that door," I boom.

"I don't listen to no motherf*ckin' man!"

I'm positioned between the carjacker and this group of women. I stand in a position to keep an eye in both directions with my rifle in hand.

"Put the stick down!" With my free hand, I slap the two-by-four to the ground. She tries to lift it. I stomp down, and it pops out of her hands.

She didn't like that. "Man, get off my stick!"

"Police! Police!" Bravo-1 yells out, and eight officers come down the hall.

The gang of women takes off, shouting obscenities and threats along the way.

Six of the officers are in plain clothes. They're Gang Squad. The remaining two are in regular uniform. They look a little greener. I tell Bravo-1 to get rid of his shotgun. We don't want any misunderstanding.

Bravo-1 moves to a different part of the building. Jogging suit is speaking to the officers about the 80-year-old man. I shoulder my rifle and engage with the officers.

"What you doin' with that?" One of the uniformed officers barks.

"What?"

"You can't have that! What is that?" He's referring to my rifle.

What it is with cops and my gun.

"It's an SKS—"

"You can't have that!"

"Yes, I can."

"Gimme that!"

I hand over the rifle. He's holding it awkwardly. He puts his finger on the trigger. It's apparent he's never handled a gun like this before.

Thank God I left the safety on.

He's making me nervous so I quickly responded, "I talked to your LT. He said it's fine."

"Oh, OK." He rolls his eyes.

The carjacker hasn't budged. He's still a threat.

"The guy behind me has a gun in his waist. He pistol-whipped the old man because three days ago, he carjacked him. Today the old man confronted him, so he hit him in the face with his gun."

"Man, we got this!" The cop snaps back.

I don't fully understand what's going on here. "The gun is in his pants."

The officer calls into his radio. He's reading the serial number on my rifle. Now, I really have no clue what's happening.

I can't help but press the issue. "Hey, this guy has a gun."

"Yeah, we got this. Back up."

A couple of gang squad officers take statements and walk the old man and jogging suit to their units. The two uniformed cops approach the carjacker. It dawns on me that they're planning to take him down.

One of the cops speaks up, "Big dog, where you stay at? Where you stay at?"

This carjacker is a thug animal. I've dealt with plenty of his kind.

He keeps his hand on the gun. His face shows panic. He's got the same suspicion I do, and he's trapped. The police and I walk the carjacker to a stairwell that leads to the basement. Four officers hang back with my rifle, talking amongst themselves.

It's a tense walk. The carjacker's face registers terror. I realize the officers' plan. They're taking him to clear space to jump him without incident.

Smart.

The cops ask him repeatedly, "C'mon big dog, where you stay? Where you stay?"

The man can hardly speak. "Over here..."

We move down the stairs. We reach the basement level. They keep prodding him with questions. "Where your apartment at?"

What's with the broken English? Are they trying to be cool with a dangerous criminal? Seems unprofessional.

The carjacker stops in front of one of the units.

"Is this your apartment?" The cops ask.

The gunman mumbles back, "yeh, yeh."

"Go on in there now."

He's not sure what's going on, and neither am I. The door opens, and he goes inside. This doesn't make any sense to me. "What's goin' on?"

The cops respond, "What?"

"I just told you he has a gun. He pistol-whipped the guy upstairs."

"Nah. Don't worry about this. We got this. Let's go upstairs."

We're back in the hall upstairs. I'm wracking my brain on the walk back. The cops continue to badger me about my weapon. "You can't be walkin' around with no rifles and stuff. It's bigger than what we got. You can't do that."

"Like I said, your lieutenant said I could."

They give up on the matter and leave. No arrests were made. No uniformed cops are in sight. Gang Squad, as far as I can tell, wasn't interested in the band of women with the two-by-four. The hall's clear. I'm not ready to leave, though.

The children I heard screaming are still inside. I knock. The door opens. Three kids are huddled inside the unit. Two of them are very young, approximately three and five years of age. Their big sister is 14. I've seen her in the hall before, sneaking out late at night. It's a one-bedroom studio in rough condition. Everything inside is past due for replacement. The old carpet appears clean. The walls have heavy paint for preservation purposes. I can smell black mold in the air. There's a bathroom on the side and one bed in the middle of the room. The mother, who's away, works three jobs. The only other piece of furniture is a big white dresser. It stands out as a nice piece.

The older sister comes forward. She tells me everything. The women that attacked them were a lesbian gang. Her little brother and sister just had their heads slammed against the frame of the door. Big sister grabbed the kids, ran in, and fought to keep the door shut. That's when the battering ram started.

When I leave, trying to piece together what just transpired and why a sergeant approaches me out in front of the building.

"Who's in charge here?"

Finally, some form of law and order will be restored here.

"I'm Dale Brown. I'm security for the building."

He eyes my rifle. "What are you doing with this gun?"

I reply, "Protecting myself and others."

"You can't have this gun!" He sounds just like the other cops, only more irate.

"Yes, I can, Sir. I talked to the lieutenant. I know my rights."

He steps in close. "Let me tell you something. You're going to get in trouble. You're supposed to be in that guardhouse."

I keep my voice restrained but firm. "Sir, I work here."

"No, you don't."

"Yes, I do."

"No, you don't!"

"Yes, I work here, sir." Above and around us, I see the tenants looking on. He's making a public show of this.

"No. You. Don't."

His name tag reads 'Goston,' "Sergeant Goston, why are you being like this when we're on the same side? Why can't we help people in this community? Why can't we work together to make it safe here with law and order?"

"We don't need your help,"

"What do you mean?"

"We don't need you. Go back to your guardhouse. And let me tell you something else. If I find out that any of y'all are knocking these doors off the hinges of these apartments, I'm coming to your house and taking your guns."

We're standing toe to toe. I'm not ready to give up.

"Well, Sergeant, I don't know what you're talking about. What I can tell you is that anybody around here that is creating a bad environment for the families —they're not going to be OK here. Sometimes doors come off hinges when drugs are being sold or people are being terrorized."

"I'm taking your guns if it happens anymore."

"Don't let any thugs live here!"

He's not having it. "You heard what I said."

I can't find the words to argue back anymore. Reluctantly, I say, "I understand."

****

The bizarre situation above was a lesson in choosing my battles. The police weren't interested in working with me. They showed the community that I wasn't a suitable liaison. What I was unaware of at the time was that, apparently, someone who looked like me, dressed like me, had taken a door off the hinges of someone close with the sergeant.

I couldn't fathom how the carjacking and beating of an old man would be tolerated by law enforcement. Why was it allowed for a group of children to be assaulted and terrorized? Why did every officer have a problem with my gun? I couldn't piece it all together. Still, I was sure that if I better understood the situation, I could successfully work with law enforcement.

One of the members of the lesbian gang was bisexual. The man in the jogging suit and her were in a relationship of sorts. However, the 14-year-old girl had been sneaking out at night to go and see him. The man was approximately 30 and courting a 14-year-old girl. That triggered action by the lesbian gang. The guy in the jogging suit used his janitor title as legal cover. He was eager to call attention to the carjacker. Cleverly, he had leveraged the situation to keep himself out of the spotlight.

*

This chapter marks a critical series of events that lead to my evolution as an agent of change. I hit a hard wall with the sergeant. I couldn't see a way around it. Without my gun, how could I provide any form of security? Without the permission and trust of the surrounding families, how could I protect them?

Chapter 9 Lessons

- Police don't like my gun.
- Lesbian gangs are a thing.
- Criminals use legal cover to circumvent trespassing laws.

10

Persons of Disinterest

Detroit, Michigan

1130 Holcomb

1130, 1160, and 1190 Holcomb Street make up a row of apartment buildings for which I provide security. During the day, I alternate between my post at the guard tower and making rounds. I explore the floors and halls of each building. I do this all day, every day, for a total of around 80 hours a week. Criminal activity runs rampant in Crack Alley. There's rarely a dull moment. The stress that these families are under never gives.

The day after the sergeant threatened to take my guns, I get a call. There's a drug dealer outside a building. I arrive at 1130 Holcomb and recognize the dealer. He's one of the managers for the building.

Dealing in front of his own place of work. Go figure.

I'm still security. I approach.

"Hey man, you can't be out here. You work here. You know better. You'll get evicted and fired."

"Oh, for real?" Three other men are out front with him. None of them look happy to see me.

I lay out their options. "These others gotta' go. They have to live here, or be inside your apartment or leave. Otherwise, it's trespassing."

The dealer doesn't put up much of a fight, but he's not happy. The men disperse, and as the drug dealer walks inside, I hear him say, "OK. You gonna' getchors'."

What's that supposed to mean?

An hour passes. At 1160 Holcomb, one building over, I spot another adult male milling around outside the front stoop. I rifle up again and head over.

"Sir, you can't stand in front of the buildings."

He's less compliant. "Ima' do what I wanna' do. You can't stop me."

I position my back against the door. He's blocked out.

"Actually, I can. You're on private property." I respond.

"You know who you f*ckin' wit? I'm a killer. I kill mother*ckas'. I kill cops. I'm a killer. Don't be messin' with my cousin out front no mo'." He looks and sounds like the rapper DMX. His tone's intense.

I reply, "You kill cops?"

"Yes, I do!"

"Turn around."

70

He turns to see a police cruiser pulling up to the scene. His breathing becomes heavy. The officers approach.

His voice cracks in desperation. "How y'all doin' officers?"

In my last dramatic voice, I say, "He said he kills cops. Just wanted to let you know."

Alarm registers on this loiterer's face, and he proceeds to give something of a stage performance.

"Officer, he lyin'! I don't know what he talkin' about. That's not true. I was just tellin' him. I love po-lices—my uncle police. I love the police. He lyin'. The security—said he was better than police. That he don't gotta listen. I said, no, nuh-uh. Nobody mess with po-lices. Not Detroit po-lices." He sounded like a menstrual performer in black face-complete with a Southern draw.

Wow. That's some fantastic acting.

The two cops look disinterested. A homeless person, a few yards away, crosses the street. The cops yell, "Hey, cross at the intersection!" They head towards the homeless jaywalker.

I run up behind the officers, "Hey, I think this guy has a weapon. He's saying he's going to kill people."

One officer glances at me. "Oh."

The two get a hold of the homeless man, put him in their squad car, and take off.

I check back with my loiterer, but he's gone.

****

The above illustrates another situation I could not have understood at the time. Life in the hood, and crime in general, are rarely, if ever, simple. Relationships, motivations, criminals, victims, and the series of events intertwine in complex ways. I later learned that the individual who resembled DMX was a sheriff's deputy. He was related to a high-ranking police officer. He was armed with a .357 magnum and a deputy's badge. The police knew who he was. Also, he was related to the previous drug dealer. The dealer, who was the building's manager, used legal cover to sell drugs. He and I both knew what he was doing, which is why he didn't make any protest.

Chapter 10 Lessons

- Criminals' acting abilities are second-to-none
- Crime and its motivating factors are never simple

11

Raid

Part 2

Detroit, Michigan

East Jefferson Avenue

The day after an actual gang of lesbians used a two-by-four as a battering ram, I get a call. The management for the apartment building I work security for is on the line.

"We need you guys to come in. There's a complaint about you by these women."

Bravo-1 and I gear up and head out. We're not sure what to expect.

We arrive, and the building managers are there. They've flown in from Florida, and it shows. One reminds me of Gloria Estefan. Her husband looks like a Cuban musician. They're well-spoken and polite. They don't fit in here. They're worried about their investment. Apparently, there's been enough daily insanity that it made its way up the grapevine.

Four of the women I met yesterday are there, too.

Laquisha is big, butch, and the ringleader of the female gang. She's putting on a show. "Der he is! He put his hands on me! He took my weapon!

He took my stick, knocked it down, and took it from me!"

The Florida couple attempts to act as a moderator. "Is that true? You took her stick?"

I speak up. "Yeah, she was ramming the door to attack some people. Her and the other women had smashed the heads of little kids against the door right before we came in. One child is three. One is five. The kids' older sister grabbed them and locked 'em inside. That's what happened."

The couple balks. They didn't know the story. "What? Wow, really?"

"Yep." "You're not gonna get that stick back." I keep my eyes on Laquisha.

"You better not touch me again." She threatened.

I'm not going to discount my safety just because she's a woman.

"If you act like a man, I'm gonna' treat you like a man."

She raises her hands as if to fight.

"If you want to fight me like a man, then I'm going to fight you like a man. If you swing, I will defend myself. I'm tellin' you now."

She looks insulted, but she's not moving. The managers are silent.

Laquisha relaxes, "OK, alright, you goin' to get yours." All four women leave the building. Everyone takes a breath. We hear dozens of tires screeching and engines revving outside. Ten cars full of people pull up.

The managers are frantic. "Who are all these people?"

I have no idea what's happening.

10 to 15 men exit the vehicles. They're upset and yelling, "Where security at! Send them mother*ckers out here. We gonna' kill them mother*ckers. We goin kill you!"

Bravo-1 and I look at each other. It's broad daylight. All the vehicles and bodies are blocking the street. No one can get in or out of the apartment. We call the police.

30 minutes pass. More cars full of thugs show up, more threats, but no police.

The mob is throwing signs, pointing, and jumping up and down. "Send security out!"

We still have no idea what's going on. The managers are terrified. I look out the window to see the mayor's mansion 300 to 400 yards away. I wonder if he can hear all this.

A call comes in. It's the lady barber. She's complaining about the cars. "I can't even park my car. My daughter is terrified. I can't get in my apartment. You guys are security. You're supposed to help us."

More calls come in. More families are making a fuss. "Where's security?"

At this point, we've called the police about ten times.

I guess you can't live forever. It's put up or shut up time.

I turn to Bravo-1. He says, "Sh*t, well, I had a good life."

We walk out.

The mob yells, "It's about to go down!"

Bravo-1 and I use Nextel radios to communicate with each other. These only transmit communication between each other. We're the only two receivers, but the mob in front of us doesn't know that.

We're in full tactical gear. Bravo-1 has his shotgun ready. My SKS is at a 45-degree angle. We move in close enough to each vehicle to see the plates. We're reading the plates as if reporting them. "Officer Johnson, the next plate reads..."

Bravo-1 can hear me reading plates to him, and he's reading plates back to me. No one else is receiving the transmission, but it's up-setting the mob. More men exit the vehicles. They're getting louder, more jumping, more hollering. We had no idea there were more.

The mob increases to about 30 angry grown men. They advance on us. They're moving at zombie speed and pressing us back toward the building. It looks like something out of The Walking Dead.

"Back up! Back up!" Bravo-1 and I are standing shoulder to shoulder. Our backs are nearly against the wall of the building. The mob forms a half-moon circle. We're pinned.

"Shoulder up!" I yell in my most authoritative militaristic voice. Bravo-1 echoes the call, "Shoulder up!"

We lift our weapons to the firing position.

"Safety off!"

"Safety off!"

Our gun barrels move side to side in a sweeping motion.

The mob threatens us further, "We gonna' kill you!" The back rows of the mob are propping up their friends and cousins, pushing them forward. "We got this! We gotchall!"

I'm aiming. There's a round in the chamber. My finger's on the trigger.

The closest members of the herd are three feet from the barrel of my rifle.

Once I start shooting, so will they.

I give a Hail-Mary warning. "If you grab the gun, you will get shot. If you come any closer, you're going to get shot. If you touch us or pull a gun, you will immediately get shot. All of you! We've got more bullets than you've got people. Our bullets will go right through all of you."

They hear me. I see anger twisting on their faces. More yelling, "We got our sh*t!"

I respond, "If I see a gun, I'm shooting! Show me a gun!"

The herd roars back, "F*ck you mother*cker, we'll kill you!"

My grip tightens.

The men rush back into their vehicles. The herd disperses. Cars' engines rev as they peel out of the street.

"We'll be back!" They yell as they speed off.

****

That marked the end of the event. I never figured out who those men were, how they organized, or what they were there for other than possibly killing me. As far as I could discern, those men had nothing to do with Laquisha and her gang. The men never did come back, either.

One might expect Bravo-1 and I did some celebrating after that. Unfortunately, we didn't have any money. So we went back to my school and continued to do tactics. We trained every day for around 12 hours. I would be dead if I resorted to idle threats, profanity, insults, or anything inciting. This event taught me a vitally important lesson.

I focused on de-escalation. Telling them to 'calm down,' attempting to appease them, or showing anything that could be perceived as weakness would not have been wise. Instead, I gave them a logical equation. In terms of my rifle's capabilities, I wasn't bluffing. 7.62 within 15 feet is very powerful. If the shooting had started, it would have been carnage. The men up front knew they'd be first. The men behind them thought they were relatively safe. Once I dismissed that notion, the group dispersed. I amplified my show of force by managing their perception. I used logic on an angry mob to persuade them to give up the cause. I didn't know mobs could be so reasonable.

Chapter 11 Lessons

- ~~Mobs cannot be reasoned with~~
- A focus on de-escalation works as a powerful neutralizer.

12

Raid

Part 3

Detroit, Michigan

East Jefferson Avenue

Approximately 3:00 PM

At my school, I have some new trainees. They're a tough group. We're working tactics when I hear screaming.

At the corner of Holcomb and East Jefferson, I see 15 women surrounding the 14-year-old girl in the middle of the day. It's the same young girl. It's the lesbian gang.

Sergeant Goston's face and words echo in my mind. *"Let me tell you something. You're going to get in trouble. You're supposed to be in that guardhouse and not in the streets...I'm taking your guns if you do anything on the city streets."*

The day after, I was surrounded by an armed and angry mob of violent men. The new trainees are in my ear. They're ready to take action. I could rifle up, grab Bravo-1, and head out with the trainees.

My chances of survival would be much higher. The odds would be more evenly stacked and unfair in my favor. The women are surrounding the 14-year-old girl. They're primarily 20s and 30s. Most of them are more attractive than average. She's an average girl, a little overweight, and with a kind personality. The young girl is the picture of innocence.

The women are yelling at her, insulting her, scaring her, and shoving her. But those women aren't surrounding me. They aren't threatening me. If I move on them, Goston will hear about it. I could lose my rifle. Without superior firepower, I won't be able to provide adequate security for anyone.

I call the police over and over. The operators tell me, "We already know. We're sending units."

The girl shrieks. They're beating her. Moderate to heavy traffic rolls through the intersection. The families in 1130, 1160, and 1190 Holcomb are watching everything go down. No one does anything.

If you don't stay in your place and keep your mouth shut, you will lose your guns.

The trainees don't understand. They're pressuring me. "C'mon. Let's go!"

The women swing a liquor bottle at the young girl's head. She ducks it. Another woman moves forward with something in her hand. It looks like a canister of some kind. She points and sprays.

The young girl falls to the ground. She's screeching, flailing, and flipping around on the pavement.

I call an ambulance. While on the phone, I see a man stepping out of the nearby liquor store while on the phone. He's the owner. He fends off the woman and takes the little girl inside.

A few minutes pass, and the ambulance rolls up. The 15 women leave and enter the building I know they live in.

In the liquor store, I see the young girl. The owner washes her face as best he can. The woman had sprayed her eyes with Raid. The flesh is burned. She's sobbing uncontrollably as we walk her to the ambulance.

It's been two hours since the attack. The girl has been rushed to the hospital. A police cruiser pulls up, and the officer steps out. I begin briefing him.

He interjects. "Where's the victim?"

"She's in the hospital."

The cop replies, "OK, have her mother take her to the precinct when she gets out."

"Don't you want to take down a report?"

"No, no victim here. Nothing we can do. What hospital was she taken to?"

"I don't know which one. The ambulance came and left. Can't you find out the hospital?"

"Our radios don't go to hospitals."

What?

I'm speechless. The officer leaves.

The next day I give the mother a call. The daughter is out of the hospital. They're both home, so I head over.

They welcome me in, and I take the lead on the conversation. "We need to go to the police department and follow up with the detectives. I have all the names of the women who did this to your daughter. I have their addresses, birthdays... It's easy. I have them all on the rent roll. We just hand in the information."

The mother interrupts. "I'm not going to press charges."

"Why not?"

"You're not from Detroit, are you?"

"I'm from Ann Arbor, but it shouldn't matter." There's a brief moment of silence. I'm losing my cool.

"The problem with Detroit is people like you who won't cooperate with law enforcement. You won't help the police help you. You just have to do your part as a citizen and a good mother."

She bites back. "The police aren't going to do anything anyway."

"Do your part, and the police will do their part. Do it like they say. Fill out the paperwork. Cooperate with investigators. Follow up. Agree to go to court, and then show up."

"It won't do any good. It will just make them angry, and they'll hurt us more."

"First of all, I'm going to protect you. The police will prosecute them. I'm a witness. There's no way they can get away with this. They can't just hurt your daughter. If you're a good mother—"

"I can't do it!"

I have to guilt this woman to do the right thing. I raise my voice. "If you were a good mother, you would do this. You would follow through."

She continues to resist. I continue to badger her.

"Fine, I'll go." She concedes.

I feel a sense of pride.

Finally, I can show a direct correlation between legal action and civilized behavior. Everyone will see those women go to jail.

The mother, the daughter, and I arrive at the police station. We walk up to the front desk.

"I'm Dale Brown. I'm security for the building.
This young lady—"

The woman behind the desk cuts me off. "Are you related to the victim?"

"No, Ma'am."

"Then, back away from my desk!"

I hear the girl sniffling. I glance back at the two women. The little girl is bandaged up like a mummy. She has one eye showing. There's a small hole in her nose. Her mouth hangs out, partially uncovered by white linen wrap.

I step away from the desk towards the little girl. "Don't cry. The officer is going to help you."

The mother and daughter look at me. I nod towards the desk, and the mother moves up.

The officer barks, "Alright, what happened?"

The mother keeps her voice low. Her posture shows fear. "My daughter getting out, umm, got out of the hospital. She was attacked—"

"She was attacked by who!"

"Umm, people in the building—"

"For what! What was the attack for!" The officer's voice rings cold.

"Well, it's—"

"Speak up!"

The little girl starts bawling. She's humiliated. She's terrified. I can't believe what is happening.

The mother glances back. We lock eyes. She's looking to me for guidance on how to proceed. I don't have an answer.

The female officer tells me to sit at a desk. I go and hear her continue to yell at the mother and daughter. When they've had enough, I offer the rent roll. The officer isn't interested.

It's over.

We're in my White Bronco, heading back to the mother's apartment. She missed her shift because of me. When we get back, I give the mother 20 dollars. It's all I have.

At home, I'm replaying the day in my thoughts. I see the girl flailing on the ground, over and over. I hear her screaming. I see myself watching it happen. The officer tells me that his radio doesn't extend to the hospitals. I see the defeated look in the mother's eyes at the precinct. The harsh tone of the officer behind the desk blares in my mind. I see sergeant Goston's face, the severity of his voice, and his words that scared me into submission. Tears of frustration well and stream down my face.

****

In this story, I met what felt like a defeat. I cried, heartbroken, in remorse and helplessness. But something else happened. Throughout this book, I share stories and the lessons I learned along with them. These are the events that detail my transformation. Everything I had been working toward was falling flat. I was becoming a victim of circumstance, just like the people I had promised to protect. While I cried and felt the shame of what I put this mother and daughter through, I made a decision. From here on, I would not allow anyone to be harmed due to my inaction.

That day, I evolved from a security person and law enforcement liaison into a **proactive** *agent of change.*

Chapter 12 Lesson

- Never let the fear of anyone or anything stop you from protecting human life.

13

Shotgun Shells and Shower Caps

Detroit, Michigan

I-94 Near Van Dyke

Approximately 4:00 PM

I-94 is just ahead. I get a call about a disturbance at 1130 Holcomb. A woman is being attacked on a stairwell.

At the scene, cop cars, a news truck, and another vehicle smashed with bullet holes. I exit my vehicle and inspect the surroundings. I notice some shell casings near the shot-up car. I recognize the black number six shotgun shells. I talk to a few witnesses to get the story.

An ambulance leaves. Police are everywhere. I hear frantic yelling. Three young African-American guys are pleading for their lives. Apparently, the cops have settled on them as the guilty party.

A reporter comes forward. "Anyone know what happened here?"

I step up. "I do."

"Do you mind being on camera?"

"Not at all."

The cameraman fixes his rig on me. The reporter extends the microphone. "What happened?"

I adopt an official tone. "I'm security for the building. The situation is that a child was shot from an elevated position from a second-floor window. It was a 12-gauge shotgun that shot a woman and baby. It was a misunderstanding that—"

Click.

The reporter and cameraman stop the interview and approach another individual. He has what looks like a clear shower cap on his head. Under that, he has Jerry Curls. I've never seen him before in the area. He speaks, and it sounds like he has rocks in his mouth.

"Iunno what happen. Somebody got shot. I seen everythang. Someone got shot ova here. Yas sir. They bullets shot somebudy. Sho nuff."

Why are they talking to him?

The reporter responds to Jerry Curls. "Thank you, sir, you've been very informative."

"You welcome!"

Who the hell is this guy?

The calls of a police officer catch my attention. "They know something, they know something!"

The young guys are protesting being arrested. They're handcuffed and put into the back of a squad car.

A woman was shot in the face and crown inside the car. She was holding a baby whose arm was almost entirely blown off.

I'm watching the police arrest three heroes. I know the three young guys came out of a Chinese food restaurant to give her first aid. They're innocent.

A plain-clothes officer is commanding the other officers.

I approach him. "I know whose shotgun shells these are. We took these shells out of a shotgun owned by Keith, the assistant manager."

He ignores me. "Grab them. Throw them in the car."

The young men are physically but non-violently resisting and begging. Once they're in the back of the squad car, they're kicking and screaming. "Please don't take me!" They're about 25 years old. The cops have brutalized them.

I continue to press the commanding officer, whose name I am sure is Lt. Clark, "Sir, can I talk to you? I'm security for the building. I know whose shotgun shells these are. I've disarmed these shells before."

Lt. Clark responds. "Nah, I don't know what you're talking about."

These young guys get dragged to jail if I don't do something. I boom in my most official TV-FBI agent voice. "Sir! These shotgun shells! I told you! Belong to that one 12-gauge!"

Lt. Clark rebuts. "What? That doesn't sound right. We already got the guys."

"No, I don't think those are the guys. The shells are underneath the window. The guy's name is Keith."

Lt. Clark has stopped paying attention. The young men are still screaming.

I up the voice from FBI agent to full-blown military drill sergeant, as gruff as I can muster without sounding like a cartoon character. "Sir! I'm telling you! These! Shells! Go to this guy!"

It gets Lt. Clark's attention. He looks up from where the shells lie. I look up. We both see someone sticking his head out the window. The head ducks back in.

The manager walks out. It's not the assistant manager Keith, who the shotgun shells belong to.

I interject before Lt. Clark can get back to ignoring me. "Ask the manager; he's right here."

Lt. Clark, in a very aggressive tone, barks at the manager. "Where's Keith?"

"I'm Keith," the manager responds.

"Don't try to be funny!" Lt. Clark's tone gets nastier. The rudeness seems overkill, even under these circumstances.

"Oh, that Keith. I'm surprised. I don't know. He's around here somewhere."

Lt. Clark picked up on the manager's deception. I must have gotten through to him.

Suddenly, a trailer park version of Jessica Simpson carrying a baby walks by. She goes into the building. She's blonde, attractive, and approximately 20 years of age. She's out of place here.

The surrounding police constitute one African-American female officer, five plain-clothes gang squad officers, and another uniformed officer. They close in on the commanding officer and the manager to find out what's happening.

The manager says, "Keith is not in his apartment. Here's what happened. This guy pinned a single mom's head to the stairs. He pushed his gun to the back of her mouth and pinned her skull to the stairs.

Children were screaming. He was kicking her between her legs. Then the guy heard someone coming down the hallway. He took off running down the stairs, went out in the front of the building, and the door closes. Keith is in the second-story window. He heard the door close and a car start. Then he started shooting."

Six officers and I go upstairs. We check Keith's apartment. He's not there. The blonde, again, walks by us in the hallway. She doesn't have her baby with her.

The female cop is scowling at her. She appears to be scowling at the whole world. It's a perpetual scowl. She's what most people would probably call plain Jane. She uses a very nasty tone with the blonde. "Where's your baby!"

The blonde stops. "'Scuse me?"

"Where is your baby!"

"I just moved in. My baby is in my apartment."

"Why is your baby not with you? Who's watching your baby?"

The blonde responds to the female cop. "Nobody's watching my baby. My baby is waiting for me."

"You left the baby by the baby by itself?"

"Yes. My baby's fine. I'm just running downstairs to check the mail."

"Ya know what. That's child endangerment. Take me to your kid right now!"

I'm getting irritated.

What does this have to do with the gunman?

The other cops are smirking and rolling their eyes. They head back downstairs.

The female cop says, "Well, I'm going with her! I'm going to find out where that baby at!"

The manager leans in close to me. He speaks in a hushed tone. "You know something, don't you?"

I don't know anything, but the manager looks very nervous.

He continues, "You know something, don't you? I had nothing to do with this. You know I had nothing to do with this."

"Well, why don't you tell me where Keith is?" I asked.

"You know something, don't you?"

"Where's Keith?" I asked again.

"I had nothing to do with this."

Trailer park Jessica Simpson opens the door to a unit with the female cop in tow. The African-American cop screams. "Get your hands up! Show me your hands!" Her weapon is drawn and pointing into the unit.

I run over and look inside. There's a large open dining room table with a baby on top of it. Underneath is a man, about 6'5", 350 pounds. His limbs are sticking out. It's Keith.

That's not really hiding. That just looks dumb.

The officers rush back. They take Keith away. He's arrested without incident.

*

Later that night, I'm watching the news report on the shooting of the woman and baby. Hair-net man appears on the screen and gives his garbled incomprehensible report. None of my coverage is shown.

Lt. Clark, as rash and brutal as he was, exhibited skilled deception detection. It revealed how easy it is to be confused about the actual sequence of events. The assistant manager and the manager of 1130 Holcomb shared the name, Keith. This kind of ability only comes with years of police experience. Lt. Clark didn't know the two managers had the same name. He didn't know for sure that any assistant manager named Keith existed at all. It was a bluff, a total feeler, and it worked.

The young blonde was another outlier. The neighborhood is 99 percent African-American. 1130 Holcomb is a very run-down apartment building. It's meager income in a crime-ridden and hazardous area.

To clear up what happened, here is how things played out. A woman living in the building was having a romantic affair with Keith, the assistant manager. He dealt drugs, mostly marijuana. It's common for people in the area, who are very poor, to exchange sex for drugs or rent. The woman's boyfriend found out about it and beat her in the stairwell while her kids, ages three and five, watched.

Keith found out, got his shotgun with the black number six shells, and went after the assaulting boyfriend while in the act. The boy-friend heard him coming and bolted. He ran down the stairs, through the hall, and out the front door. Keith was on the second floor, heard the front door open and shut, and a car started. Keith assumed it was a getaway car and the boyfriend was inside. What happened is that the boyfriend immediately turned right or left once he was outside the building. The vehicle, which had a woman and infant inside, likely saw the gun-toting boyfriend barreling toward them.

Like the young men who were brutalized and falsely accused, she was there to get food from a nearby Chinese restaurant. Keith shot the car multiple times as she was driving away from the second story. He stopped the car and severely injured the woman and baby. He was trying to avenge the woman in the stairwell.

Keith did time in jail, but not very much. He was only in jail for about three months. The courts saw his actions as an effort to pro-tect someone's life. In my mind, had he not been selling drugs or trading rent for sex with a woman who already had a boyfriend, none of this would have happened.

Hair-net man, to this day, I wonder about. I had never seen him before, and I never saw him again. I had been calling the news stations for five years before the incident occurred. For every shooting and every crime, I contacted the news network. I hoped that news coverage of these occurrences might motivate the police to take more notice. Never once did the news networks show up. I couldn't help but feel very insulted by the reporter's decision to go with sensationalism instead of the truth.

Violence is punished with violence, and the story behind it is always complicated. I heard later that the assistant manager Keith was murdered by the friends or family of the woman and baby. Criminals in Detroit who are criminal informants, related to police officers, or are protected by the police for many reasons, often die this way. The people of Detroit don't expect justice from the system.

Chapter 13 Lessons

- Experienced cops have skilled powers of perception
- The news is often inaccurate and sensationalized
- Innocent heroes are at risk of arrest.

14
The Chef in 202

Detroit, Michigan

April 1996

Hibbard and East Jefferson

Approximately 6:00 PM

I'm training new team members in tactics at my school, the Institute of Survival Technology, or 'IST' for short. There's a knock at the front door. A young woman, approximately 25 years of age, is there. She's attractive with long hair, somewhat voluptuous. She looks like she might work in the entertainment field, possibly as a dancer. She's crying.

"Where were you!"

I've never seen this woman before in my life. "What do you mean?"

"You guys do security for the building?"

"Yes, ma'am."

"Why didn't you help my sister? She knew it was you! She could hear your voice!"

I'm sympathetic, this woman is trembling with rage, but I have no idea what's happening. "What are you talking about, ma'am?"

"Yesterday! You were at her door. Why couldn't you help her? She was naked on the floor, being beaten, robbed, and raped! She was screaming!"

There was an incident that happened a day prior, but I had no idea these things happened to her sister. I do my best to apologize, but I'm heartbroken and ashamed.

I tell the woman I'm going to take action immediately.

*

The day before, at Hibbard and East Jefferson, I was locking up the training center for the day. It's at the bottom of a 15-story building known as the Hibbard Apartments. It's a beautiful building. Concrete gargoyles mount the roof, art deco, ancient tile work, and antique elevators with sliding doors. It's the kind of place you'd expect to see Humphrey Bogart hanging around.

Unemployment doesn't exist in this building. The median income of the residents runs from thirty thousand to forty thousand dollars a year. Some incomes are as high as 60 to 75,000 a year. The building has townhouses located on the upper floors and penthouse suites.

While locking up, I spot a police car. Two officers are climbing into the vehicle.

I flag them down. "Do you need to get in the building?"

The officer responds, "Yeah, we got a call about a woman running down the hallway naked, screaming for help, banging on doors. Second floor. We couldn't get in the building so, we're leaving."

"Well, I have the key."

We head to the second floor and stop in front of unit 202. I don't hear any screaming. Nobody is running up and down the halls. The two officers stand in front of the door. I look at them. They look at me.

No one steps up to knock on 202. I step forward, give a light knock, and step back.

No one comes to the door. One of the officers bangs on the door with a flashlight.

"Detroit Police."

We hear movement behind the door. It opens a little, no more than four inches.

All I can see is a bit of the man's face. He's African-American, clean-shaven, and professional, with short hair and caramel skin. He's approximately 45 years of age, and he's breathing heavily. Sweat glistens on his skin, and there's a half-inch cut near his nose. A trickle of blood runs down his cheek. This guy looks weird to me, but I assume the cops know what to do.

One officer speaks. "Uh, sir. Did you call the police about a woman running and screaming naked down the hallway? Or something?"

The man behind the door pants, "No. I didn't call anyone. I didn't call anyone."

The officer responds. "OK."

We walk away and approach a Bolivian lady in the hall. She works as a cleaning lady in the building. She and her family are residents. She speaks in broken English to the two officers and me. "Girl. Running. Hallway. Black girl. Running. Screaming. Yelling 'help.' Hitting door. Man grab her. Pull her down hallway."

The officer says, "Well, OK."

We leave the lady to her business, and the cops turn to each other. "Nothing going on here."

The three of us head down the stairs to exit the building. One officer turns to me. "That's cool." He indicates my rifle, the SKS. "Can I check it out?"

I hand off my rifle. He inspects it. "This is cool.

He's inspecting the scope, laser sight, flashlight, 30-round magazine, folding stock, and big muzzle brake. It is impressive looking, and it's very cheap. I know there's no bullet in the chamber. He hands it back, and the officers leave the building.

*

The next day, the young woman's sister was in front of me. She's upset, crying, screaming, and furious with me. I realize her sister was just on the other side of the door, likely praying that the cops and I would have kicked the door in and rescued her. Instead, we walked away.

I head upstairs, march straight to unit 202, and bang on the door.

The same clean-shaven man I met the day before opens the door.

I challenge him. "What's this all about?"

He plays dumb, and I explain what I've been informed of.

He continues to defend himself. "I don't know. She was lying. We went on a date. I don't know what she's talking about."

"You have no idea?" I asked.

"No. I'm a chef at a really nice restaurant downtown."

Something is wrong with this story.

I don't understand yet. I tell him I'll be back and speak with the apartment management.

I explain the situation to a lady in the management office. She responds, "I don't know about this situation, but I know he got arrested before for abducting a woman. He went to prison."

"What!"

I'm back upstairs. I'm pounding on the door again. The chef opens the door.

"You abducted a woman and went to prison?"

"Yeah, that was a long time ago. I don't do that anymore."

"I don't know what this is. But you better not have any more of these kinds of situations. You better not let me find out that anything like this happens again. Nothing. There can't be anything."

"It didn't happen. She's lying."

"But you had another abduction before?"

"That was a long time ago! I'm a chef! I don't know why she would lie."

"This is unacceptable. Abducting women is not something we're going to have here. You understand? If I ever get any reports about you abducting a female again, it's going to be a serious problem."

"You're not going to get any reports like that because I'm not doing anything like that."

The chef is articulate. He's highly educated. His story is convincing. He's either an excellent liar, or I'm missing something. I make a decision.

"I hear what you're saying, but I don't believe you. You abduct women, go to prison, and now someone is accusing you of doing this to her sister. But you didn't do it?"

"No, I didn't do that! We were dating, and she got an attitude—"

I interrupt. "Nope. Nope. No. You know what? You better not let me find out that you ever do anything like that again. Nothing. No innuendo. No insinuation. Nothing."

"You won't be. I don't have these kinds of problems."

"OK, man. I'm sick of this guy. Whatever. You heard what I said, though?"

"Yes."

I call the police. I wait. They don't show, so I head to the station. I attempt to start an investigation, but the front officers aren't working with me. No investigation happens. I'm not the victim.

This guy is a licensed chef working at a well-known high-end restaurant. He's bringing in around 60,000 dollars a year. He's abducting women and getting away with it.

*

Two weeks later, I receive a call from another woman who lives in the chef's building. She's frantic. "Please help me. I've been beaten, attacked."

I meet her, and she's not kidding.

"He attacked me! Tried to rape me! Beat me! Look at my face. It's messed up!"

She's approximately 50 years of age. She's professional and works as a manager in an office somewhere. She's upset but has a pleasant demeanor. Her face is bloodied and swollen. The eyes are puffy and bloodshot. A tooth is missing.

She continues, "My sons are angry. They're coming over here. They're going to kill him. He attacked me and wouldn't let me out. I had to fight to get out of there, ripping my clothes and raping me. It was horrible."

I know she's called the police. I know they aren't doing anything. She doesn't understand why, and neither do I.

I head to the police station and make a report. I have to keep on this guy.

When I pull in and exit my vehicle, I see the chef in the passenger seat of a large Cadillac pulling up.

The driver is huge. He's approximately 6'6", 300 pounds, filling the car.

I step forward and yell. "Get out of the car!"
"What?" The chef calls back.

"Sir, you need to step out of the car."

The larger, very dark complected driver yells back. "Don't threaten my friend!"

"Sir, this has nothing to do with you. I'm *definitely* going to threaten this individual."

"Don't threaten my friend, or I will get out of the car."

"This has nothing to do with you. Don't get out of the car."

I focus back on the chef. "You need to step out. I told you if you attack women in these buildings—I told you that I was going to attack you, right? I told you that, right?"

"I'm not getting out."

The driver yells at the chef. "You still doin' that? You still attackin' women, man? Get the f*ck out my car. Get the f*ck out my car! You told me you don't do that no more. Get the f*ck out!" He begins pushing the chef against the passenger door. The door opens.

I grab the chef and hip-toss him to the pavement—his body slams against the concrete.

Looking down at him, I say, "You wanna get up and fight me? Get up and put your hands up."
He raises his hands in protest. "No, no, please."
I drop my hands and lean in close. I speak with a steady tone. "Here's what's going to happen. I'm going to let you off the ground. When I let you off the ground, you have 24 hours to get out of the building. 24 hours. Do you understand?"

"Yes."

Twenty-four hours later, the chef is gone. The police still haven't done anything regarding either of the women recently attacked.

*

A few days later, I run into the businesswoman. "I was feeling terrorized in my own building. Thanks to you, he's completely gone. I can sleep at night. Thank you."

*

More time goes by, and I hear more stories about the chef. More abductions, more harassment, more attacks. Then, six months go by.

*

I'm standing outside the building. I spot a station wagon driving southbound on Hibbard. It turns east onto Jefferson. I recognize the same businesswoman in the passenger seat. She's banging against the window, arms flailing, and yelling for help. I don't recognize the driver.

I pull out my Nextel Raven cellular phone. It's a military-grade phone, waterproof, and very durable. In 1996, these aren't common. I call 911.

"This is security for the building! Lady abducted! Jefferson!"

The operator responds. "They're moving?"

"Yes!"

"Where they going?"
"I don't know! He's taking her. He's taking her!"

"Well, we don't respond to situations that are moving."

There's a pause.

"What?"

"We can't do anything about that. It's moving. He's moving. There's nothing we can do."

Wow. Wow, I guess there's nothing I can do either.

The car speeds out of sight.

*

Days later, the business lady returns. She confronts me again. I'm ashamed again. She's not happy, but she's not hostile. "Did you call the police? Did you tell them?"

"I did. They wouldn't respond to the situation."

"I had to do what I had to do. My ex-husband abducted me, beat me, raped me, tortured me for days. I just got out. I just escaped him. He's just not letting go. Why didn't you help me, though? You saw me."

"I would if I could. My car was around the block."

An indignant look spreads across her face. I see she's clearly hurt, but she's had enough confrontations.

***

In the series of events above, I discovered that the chef had argued that the women were prostitutes. This is a common accusation violent criminals make. It works, too. Police and regular people often believe it. Dealing with a more educated and affluent criminal posed some new challenges. In the end, the sister who approached me at the school was more convincing. In addition, the chef had a history of criminal activity.

When I first confronted the chef, my mistake was assuming that the police officers would be able to read the situation. They didn't want to be there. They weren't interested. They showed reluctance from the very start. The police and I failed to 'READ' (Recognize Evasive Aggressive Deceptive Behavior) the situation. In the end, I got him out of the building by taking matters into my own hands. Still, I feel for the woman being raped and brutalized on the other side of the door. It still haunts me.

While I was baffled by the police's response regarding the business-woman in the station wagon, I will admit that it is a difficult situation to address. Shooting a gun within city limits brings with it a host of problems. I was armed then, but opening fire on the station wagon or attempting to shoot out the tires would have resulted in legal problems. Surrounding families would have protested, stating that I was firing toward their property and around their families.

Chapter 14 Lessons

- ~~Educated men do not commit violent crimes.~~
- "Moving" situations leave limited options.
- Call for police assistance, but don't be dependent on police actions as they might not be able to be there on time.

15
Family Matters

Detroit, Michigan

July 1996

East Jefferson, Institute of Survival Technology

I'm teaching, training, and working on tactics. It's easy to train all day when you're broke. An older couple enters through the front door of my school. The woman is upset.

I approach, and she speaks first. "Can you help us upstairs?"

She knows I'm security for the parking lot and the building.

"Please, help us! My son is drunk, on probation, he has a knife. He has the knife to my Godson's throat. He's threatening to stab him. We don't want tem killed. We can't call the police. We don't want them killed by the police."

"OK, I'll go up there and see what I can do. But we have to call the police."

And we do. I call. Then I head up to their unit. The parents open the door for me, and I step inside.

A young man, approximately 25 years old, 180 pounds, and about 5'10", is lying in the middle of the floor. His hands are tucked under a pillow he's face-down on. It looks like he's pretending to be asleep. Another young man is lying on the couch. He's frozen with fear, staring right at me.

I try a friendly voice. "Hey, how's it going?"

No answer. I leap into the air toward the young man on the floor. *He can't hear my footsteps approaching if I'm in the air.* I land nearly on top of him. He rolls over, and a 12-inch kitchen knife emerges from under the pillow.

I pin his elbows, invert his arm, and remove the blade. He's not going anywhere now.

The family and I keep our positions until the police arrive. They do and take the young man into custody. The family is happy.

***

I met the young man five years after the story above occurred. I was in a nightclub when he approached. I didn't recognize him, and he had a hard time believing that.
He wasn't pleased with me.

He had gotten five years in prison for violating his parole. As seen in previous chapters, once people go to prison and get out, they tend to remember who put them there.

My life wasn't my priority in doing what I was doing. The lives of the surrounding families were. I didn't expect to live into a ripe old age doing what I was doing. There were times when I thought it was impossible that I would survive based on my mission and the circumstances.

Chapter 16 Lessons

- Violating probation can earn you years in prison
- Criminals remember who is responsible for their incarceration.

16
The Boy Next-Door

Detroit, Michigan

August 1996

Holcomb Arms Apartment

The Holcombs Arms Apartment building has three floors. Two are above ground; one is below. There are 30 units in total. After dealing with what I suspect is a Nazi war criminal in the building's basement, I get a call.

It's about a new girl in the building. I've met her in passing in the halls before. She's European-American, attractive, and very friendly. Her boyfriend is a firefighter.

The manager is on the line. "Dale, I need you to go over there. There's a threat. This girl just moved in."

I arrive at the young lady's unit. She answers and produces a letter. The letter is in what looks like a sandwich bag. "This was left under my door. I called the police; they didn't show up." She says.
Her boyfriend is there, and he's upset. Not even he can believe that the police aren't doing anything.

I read the letter. I tell her, "I have no idea who this could be."

She responds, "I think it could be the guy next door. He's weird. He keeps knocking on my door and asking questions.

I knock on the neighbor's door. A young African-American guy steps forward. He's approximately 20, athletic, and I can see he's odd right away.

I start off friendly, "Hey, how's it going?"

"Fine, fine."

"Did you see anything strange recently? There was a note left at the door of your neighbor next-door."

"Oh, she's really nice. I know her. I've met her. She's really nice."

His speech is off. I suspect some kind of mental disorder. His level of concern seems inappropriate; too pleasant.

This guy is attempting to be deceptive.

He continues, "Man, that's crazy what's goin' on with that lady next-door."

"Yeah, it is, isn't it?"

"Yeah, she just moved in!"
"Yeah, I know. It's crazy. Who would write those things? You know what I mean?" I respond

"Yeah, it's crazy. To write those things that are written in that letter are crazy."

"Right. What did it say?" I ask.

"Oh, it's talkin' about raping her and killing her and stuff like that?"

I pause for a beat. "How do you know it said that?"

He pauses. His mind is clearly racing. "Didn't you say it?"

"No, I didn't say anything."

"No, I dunno. I dunno how I know."

I lean in a little closer. "You know how you know what's in that letter, don't you?"

"No, I don't know. I dunno how I know."

I don't have this guy yet.

I tell him to hold on and go back to the young lady.

"Did you talk to him? Did you show him the letter?"

"All I did was ask him if he knows who put the letter under my door. That's all I said."

"Alright."

I knock on the young guy's unit. He opens the door.

Calmly, I ask. "So, you put the note under the door."

Like a five-year-old caught lying, he deflates. "...yes."

I head-butt him in the chest. He falters back a few steps.

"Get your things, and get out of the apartment. You have to leave. Call your family. They have to come get you."

A few minutes later, my phone rings. It's the guy's sister. All I can hear is yelling and profanity through the receiver.

Once she takes a breath, I speak up. "You have a choice. You can leave him there, and he's going to go to prison. Or you can keep him in your custody and control. Because he's going to do something to someone, or he's going to get hurt. He can't be by himself, obviously."

The sister responds, "You're right. You're right."

The next day, the young man's family shows up, and he's out of the building. Shortly after, the female neighbor was gone too.

***

In this story the young lady was so traumatized by the horrific things in the letter that she moved out that same day. The note went into gross detail on how he planned to rape and kill her. He was clearly sick.

It didn't take much detective work to get him to tell on himself. Once I realized something unusual about his speech pattern and suspected deception, I adopted a positive tone. He was a young guy, not much younger than me. Being buddy-buddy got him to drop his guard.

Chapter 16 Lessons

- Closely examine speech patterns and tone of voice in a potentially confrontational situation.

17
Scared Silent

Detroit, Michigan

November 1996

My home is in a 17-story building that's across from the Jeffersonian. I'm sitting down when I hear someone screaming outside. It sounds like a man yelling. I grab my shotgun, a Mossberg 590 tactical, and step out.

Next to a truck is the man. He has a shotgun, too. Mine is on a strap held vertically against my back. If you're looking straight at me, you can't see the gun.

The truck's a white Chevy, very small, S-10, and beat up. The man is approximately 55 to 60. He's dark-complected and violently screaming, "I will f*ckin'in' kill you!" over and over. "You lil' b*tch!" over and over.

He appears to be yelling at the building and no one in particular.

"Sir, who are you talking to?"

"Mind your own business. This has nothin' to do with you."

"Sir, you've got a shotgun. I am security. You're threatening people here. I've already called the police."

He starts paying more attention to me. I start moving laterally towards the street, away from him at an angle. How I'm positioned, he can now see my shotgun.

The truck takes off.

I turned towards the building to guess which unit he was yelling at. I see a woman sticking her head out of one of the windows ten stories up. After doing the math to ascertain which unit she's in, I head up and knock on the door.

She answers and is eager to speak to me. "Can you help me?"

"What do you need?"

"My daughter. There's something wrong with her. She's non-responsive."

The girl is 14 years old. She looks healthy, like an athlete. She's well-mannered, wearing conservative clothes. Her hair is nicely done. She looks like a typical suburban middle-class teenager. Her mother looks like an ordinary working-class mom.

"We just need help. Please."

"Well, ma'am, what's wrong? What was that guy yelling about?"

"It's a long story, but he's threatening to kill my daughter."
"What do you mean?"

"He shot at her before. And now he's scared she's going to testify in court against him tomorrow. He's saying he's going to kill her if she testifies. He's my ex-boyfriend, and he doesn't understand that the police are making her testify. There's nothing we can do. We have to go to court tomorrow, and he owns this apartment. He could come in here anytime because it's in his name. He's a manager for Ford Motor Company. He wants to kill her. That's why he had the shotgun. He said if she disagreed, he would come to kill her right now. She's so scared she can't speak."

The girl is standing up, looking straight ahead.

I approach. "Hello? Hello, are you OK?"

She doesn't respond.

"Can you please help my daughter? Can you please take her somewhere she can be safe?"

"OK, I'll take her in with me and my ex-wife. She can stay with us."

"Please take her right now. He has a set of keys."

We walk down to my unit on the second floor. The girl doesn't say a word in the hallway and nothing in the elevator. Her eyes are wide open. She's in some kind of state of shock.

I bring her into my unit. My ex-wife's home, and I explain. She's not into it, which surprises me because she's a very religious Christian woman. She goes to church five days a week. I explain the situation again. This girl is going to stay with us just for a few days.

"No, I don't want to do that."

"I don't understand. You're a person of faith. Why would you not want to take care of someone who needs help?"

"Because this is our house. This is our home. We don't bring people here."

"We are definitely going to take care of her."

On the first day, the girl is non-communicative. She's not eating. She sleeps a lot.

The next day, she starts talking to my ex-wife. We keep the atmosphere very positive for the young lady, but she looks fatigued. Once she starts eating, she starts telling stories. We ask about the situation.

"He tried to attack me. I resisted, and he shot at me."

She gives more details. It was a sexual assault. The police got called, and once they got her story, they arrested him. He's being charged with attempted murder. Additionally, the man is married with children. The woman and daughter are something of a side family. He's likely to lose everything if she testifies, his job, family, and freedom. The man likely makes six figures.

By the end of the second day and on the third day, the girl has completely transformed. She's outgoing and cheerful. I'm even hearing her laugh some.

***

I didn't accompany the mother and daughter to the courthouse, but I knew she went. I don't know what happened to the man. The mother and daughter ended up moving out of the area, which was definitely a good idea.

Never had I seen someone go into such a state of shock. It was shocking to witness how this young lady was affected by her mother's boyfriend's attack. As I think of the millions of kids being attacked every day I'm glad I was able to help one.

My wife at that time, now ex-wife, was reserved at first out of fear that the man may attack us for protecting her. I reminded her that this is a young lady who needs our help. I explained that this was the purpose of my organization. Even though she was a very religious person, she was very reluctant. Perhaps she realized that this is part of her faith. She ended up counseling and praying with the young girl until she felt safe and returned to her normal self.

Chapter 17 Lessons

- ~~Wealthy people do not commit violent crimes.~~
- The impact of an attack from an adult to a child is potent
- Protection is the foundation required for a good quality of life
- You can prevent a murder by protecting the victims from the attackers.

18
Wheels of Fury

Detroit, Michigan

I bought a white Ford Taurus for 250 dollars. It was to be my first patrol car. It's four cylinders. There's no transmission. It maintains a speed of 35 miles per hour and sounds like a moped.

I made a sign at Kinko's, laminated it, and duct-taped it to the door. Then I mounted a yellow light on top, plugged it in, and hit the neighborhood streets.

On my first patrol, I see a car pull up in a parking lot. A young guy gets out, approaches a different vehicle, and smashes the window. The yellow light starts flashing, and I head straight for him. He didn't see me beforehand.

An older man in a security uniform comes hobbling up. He's taking action.

I yell out the window, "Hold that kid right there!" I look at the kid, "Don't move!"

These guys are here stealing cars. The car that the kid was in takes off. Another nearby car peels out and follows behind the first.

The two vehicles gun it down a neighborhood street.

The engine is whining. I floor it and slowly accelerate to 35 miles per hour. The two cars ahead of me must go 50 or 60 miles per hour. They are leaving me.

I watch their taillights turn down another street, and I give chase.

It doesn't look like a dead end. In the distance, I think I see an outlet.

The first car slams on its brakes. I hear the tires screech and see the brake lights. It starts to back up. The next car accelerates toward the leading vehicle while it's in reverse.

The follow-car collides with the first one, bounces off, and hits a tree. Both cars are trashed; totaled. Both cars are completely stopped. The street was a dead end.

Wow.
I hang a right and return to the parking lot.

*

A year later, a young guy approaches me at a nightclub. "You re-member me?"

I take a hard look. "Nope."

"Man, I went to prison because of you!"

"What are you talking about?"

"I broke a window. That's all I did. I broke a glass window, that's all

I did! And they put me away for a year and a half!"

"That is kind of harsh compared to a lot of crimes I know about. Um. Sorry."

"Nah, f*ck that!" He walks away.

I guess he spoke his peace.

***

In this short story, you can see how reactive criminals can be when caught. One and a half years is quite a long time for breaking a window, even if it is related to auto theft.

One car was a getaway car, and the other was a stolen vehicle. I later met the woman who owned the vehicle with the shattered window. She was a single mom; she was heartbroken. Detroit winters are freezing. She was concerned about how to get to work. She didn't have any money. I didn't have any money. There wasn't much that I could do.

Chapter 18 Lessons
- Criminals fear white cars with lights on the top
- ~~Sentences always match the crime~~
- Dead ends don't always look like dead ends

19
The Shooting of
Icon-1

Detroit, Michigan

October 1996

Icon-1 is from Ann Arbor, Michigan, the same as myself. His real name is Terry, but I didn't know him in school. We were in junior high together.

On paper, it's easy to miss a lot about Icon-1. His family owns an art gallery in Ann Arbor. His sister became a high-end attorney who works in a Detroit office.

Myself and Icon-1 head over. A grocery store, Food Express, recently hired us. The owner informs us that senior citizens are being attacked regularly by gang members and violent criminals. I sign myself and Icon-1 in, and we start working.

The owner takes a hard look at Icon-1. "I don't want him working here. He's too skinny. No way he can protect anyone."

It's true. Icon-1 is about 5'11 and 120 pounds. He's not the physically intimidating presence you'd expect in a security guard.

I stick up for him. I try to get across to the owner how capable he is.

"Just too skinny."

"He knows what he's doing." I reply.

"He can't work anymore after today." He continues.

I concede.

Later in the shift, a scuffle calls our attention. An older woman is being attacked.

Icon-1 is closer to the scene and bolts in before I can.

A large man grabs an 80-yeard old lady. She's clinging to her purse and her food stamps. He hits her face with his fist repeatedly. I can see the blood around her eyes, nose, and mouth.

Icon-1 grabs the striker. Applies a sleeper hold.
The man is taken to the ground and rendered unconscious within seconds.

At the end of our shift, the owner approaches. He requests — no— *requires* Icon-1 to provide security to the store from now on.

Icon-1 loved to train. We'd go on for 10 hours a day of tactics, martial arts, sticks, knives, firearms, disarms, and takedowns. A few weeks later, I'm surprised when he calls out of work. He says his stomach hurts. I probe a bit.

"You know we protect people?"

"Yes."

"We are expected to protect people. Someone could shoot us in the stomach, and we still have to protect. We have to be able to go through bullets to protect people."

He concedes.

It's Friday night. Bravo-1 decided earlier that he wanted to work by himself at a nightclub. That's not in line with our protocol, but if my team members are willing to acknowledge and accept the risks that working alone entails fully, then I tend to slide on the rules now and then. Bravo-1 had pushed me hard on this one for whatever reason.
The club was well-known. It was internationally recognized for the caliber of entertainers it brought in. Famous comedians frequented this particular club along with extravagantly dressed men and women.

Bravo-1 is working the club while Icon-1 and I head to a different assignment. Unlike Icon-1, Bravo-1 brings with him an intimidating presence. He's 6'4 and has 280 pounds of solid muscle. He resembles Ultra Man for anyone familiar with the character.

At the Nile Nightclub, a gang pushes through the club's back door. They turn aggressive, and Bravo-1 intervenes. The security guards in place, the Nation of Islam, often referred to as X-Men, move them back out. But they're not happy.

Fifteen gang members surround Bravo-1 outside. They get loud and threatening.

Bravo-1 is well-trained in fighting a large group of people and is very, very strong. He's able to strike in multiple directions repeatedly. He moves laterally and continuously, making it very difficult for multiple individuals to converge on him.

Gang members are swinging at him and hitting each other. Bravo-1 slams a couple of heads together when the opportunity presents itself. Every offensive action he takes directly hinders a gang member's ability to stand, breathe, or see.
One gang member moves in and gets caught in a chokehold.

The police, who like to gawk at the girls who frequent the club, is out front. Bravo-1 physically hands one of the gang members over to two cops. The gang member breaks free of the cops, grabs an orange construction barrel, and charges straight at Bravo-1's back. He heads back inside the building.

"Look out!"

Bravo-1 turns. The barrel collides with his nose and mouth and knocks him off his feet. His skull bangs against the door. The barrel drops, and Bravo-1 jumps to his feet.

The gang member backs away to use the crowd of his fellow gang members as cover.

Bravo-1 charges through the blocking members. He grabs the assaulter, tosses him to the ground, and jumps on his head. This is known as a 'curbie.'

The other members leave, along with the police.

Bravo-1's shift ends a few hours later. I still have my 1995 White Bronco 2 with the logo on the side and the words "Survival Instructor."

"I never let anyone drive my car, but I'll let you. I'm with Icon-1 at another location. I need you to pick up Bravo-1 working at The Nile Club and bring him back here for our next assignment."

Icon-1 heads out to pick up Bravo-1. He arrives, but Bravo-1 is not up for another assignment.

"I'm in a bad mood. Drop me off. I'll take the bus home."

Icon-1 pulls the Bronco over near a bus stop, and Bravo-1 departs.

Icon-1 sits there on his phone while the engine's running.

He notices someone crossing the street. He looks back down, then back up. The man is running straight towards him and firing a nine-shot revolver. The window shatters. Bullets thud into the side of the vehicle.

Icon-1 hit's the gas. He throws his arm up to block the bullets and heads north on East Jefferson towards Lafayette, near his home. The shooter is running alongside the Bronco firing. But he doesn't turn the corner. The last thing Icon-1 remembers is turning the corner.
The car rides up onto the grass and smashes into a car.

A nurse, who just ended a shift treating gunshot wounds, comes running out to see who hit her car. She finds Icon-1 in the white Bronco. She grabs a blanket, tosses it over his head, and applies pressure on the wounds.

A black S.U.V. pulls up. A man rolls the window down. "Is he OK?"

The nurse responds. "No. He's shot a lot."

The man in the S.U.V. says, "I'm going to get the police," and zooms off.

I'm at Cafe Mahogany, a jazz club when I get a call from Icon-1's phone number. I answer.

"Dis, da po-lice. Yo man down."

You've got to be kidding me.

"Sir, who are you, and how did you get this device?"

"Dis da po-lice, I jus' tol' you. Yo Man down."

"Sir, posing like a police officer is a criminal offense. However, I will give you 50 dollars cash to return my phone."

The phone has 100-dollar insurance on it.

"I ain't gonna' tell you again!"

I gather directions and arrive at the scene. The guy, despite his vernacular, is a police officer.

The police didn't canvas the area. They don't talk to the homeowners.

We're across the street from where Rosa Parks once lived. I realize if she still lived there, she would have seen Icon-1 get gunned down and bleeding outside her window.

I head to the hospital, where Icon-1 was taken.

Icon-1's mother and sister are standing over him in his room. My mother shows up as well. We make somber greetings and give hugs. I approach my fallen teammate. He has a breathing tube, but he's awake. He's writing something down on a piece of paper. He hands it to me. I read: 'I lost my awareness.'

***

Icon-1 was hospitalized for five days with a tube down his throat and several months later, he was released from the hospital. When he got out, he lost movement in his left hand and mobility in his left leg. Before the shooting, he was one of the most impressive martial artists I have ever seen!

Instead of the standard military fade haircut we all maintained every week, now his dreadlocks hang down to nearly the entire length of his body, approximately five feet. On several occasions during training, I watched him run toward a well, then up the wall, spin 180 degrees, and spring off the wall. All of this was done while fluidly wielding a sword. It was like watching a Chinese sword master and was nothing short of amazing. He's still alive today.

Icon-1 was shot seven times. He told me that he used his chi in the hospital to overcome the pain of the bullets. Six months after, he was training in martial arts again.

When I had re-entered the scene, I found a few witnesses. One stated that the man in the black S.U.V. was the shooter—a man I had met before and is head of a gang from Chicago. I told them they couldn't enter one of the apartment buildings I was employed for protection. They, of course, weren't happy about that. While leaving the premises, one of the men said, "You don't know who you're f*ckin' with. You're going to regret this."

The shooting of Icon-1 may not have had anything to do with the gang members or the events that had occurred with Bravo-1 at The Nile Club earlier that night. Icon-1 had been driving my car. The man may have been a hitman sent to kill me and was trying to confirm the kill by questioning a nurse.

When I saw the shooter the next day, he looked more than a little surprised to see me.

Chapter 19 Lessons

- In a fight, training and ability outweigh size.
- When fighting multiple people at once, never stop moving in a circle.
- Awareness is your first and most important line of defense.
- Criminals often attach your identity to your vehicle.

20
Urban Gardening

Detroit, Michigan

August 1998

I receive a call about a man bleeding in a hallway. The cops get called, and I head over. The man who stabbed the guy is said to be in the building.

 On the way to see family, I'm in shorts and a tank top.

We've got a portable camera. It's 8mm, has a rotating lens on the right side, and a connected four-inch screen. A 10-year ex-cop named Hinderman is with me when I arrive.

"Hold this." I hand it off to my ex-cop team member and a bag carrying my gun, a Ruger p90-45 semi-automatic pistol.

An older man stands in the vestibule, pressing his hand against his neck. Blood gurgles from his throat and runs down his arm.
He's just standing there.

About 15 women and kids gawk at us from 10 flights of surrounding stairs. The vestibule itself measures approximately 30 by 30 feet.

Another man, gray-haired, walks by with a cane. He's known to be trouble and recently got out of prison for murder.

I've seen him shuffle around the area with that cane, but he's not walking like he usually does. I approach. He's moving very well; lively event.

"Hey, how's it goin'? Everything OK?"

He looks at me. "Get out of my way."

"What's goin' on here?"

"Nothing, *Dale*."

How does he know my name?

The man's hand drops to his side out of my line of sight. He's approximately 5'7", 200 pounds, medium build, dark-complected, very aggressive demeanor, and he speaks with a southern drawl.

"You better get out my way, or we gonna' buck."

"Wait a minute, just stand by. The police will be here in a moment. Everything will be fine; you can explain everything when they get here. But you can't leave until the police arrive."

I glance over at the man holding his bloodied throat. The guy in front of me keeps his hand out of sight. He's fidgeting with something behind his leg.

The women and children along the stairs above are pointing at him.

The old guy spins around. They stop pointing and look away at the walls and nothing in particular.

"If you don't bring your hands where I can see them, I'm about to put you on the ground."

"I ain't gonna' tell you one more time to get out my way, Dale, or we gonna' buck."

His hand moves.

Hinderman starts screaming, "He's got a knife! He's got a knife!"

I step in, slash my forearm forward into him, and simultaneously push his head back.

Realizing he won't be able to extend the blade, he lets out a high-pitched yell.

His entire energy changes. He's trying to escape now.

He grabs onto the stairs to keep from going down to the ground. I flip his head back and bring him into a complete takedown.

From a kneeling position, I look up. The camera Hinderman is holding is pointed straight at me. I smile while holding the disarmed knife in a dominating pose.

This is the most significant day ever. I now have an actual real-life knife disarm, and, nobody has that. Almost nobody in the world has that but me. I have raised the bar of martial arts training. I'm going to be in a magazine for martial arts. I'm going to change the world. I'm going to bein a movie just about martial arts where I disarm a knife in real life. I'm on my way to Hollywood. This is it.

The police show up. I'm excited.

Two officers come forward. "OK, what happened?"

"Yes, sir, I got a situation. I actually have a video. Let me show you the video. I disarmed him, here's his knife. The great thing is I have it on video."

"What?"

"Yes, that's right, officer. I have an actual takedown and disarm of a knife-wielding aggressor, in which I did not hurt him."

"Really?"

"Yes, let me show you!"

Proudly, I play the video.

I appear on the screen. The camera is on my back. It shows me moving forward. The sound of Hinderman screaming, "He's got a knife! He's got a knife!" comes through the audio. Then the camera pans down to the ground. All we can see is cement. The camera pans back up, and I'm on the screen holding the knife over the guy, smiling. The footage shows the other guy holding the knife or attempting to attack me at no point. Just me attacking him. Just me, holding the knife.

I turn off the camera. "Never mind that. The people on the stairs are witnesses."

Without hesitation, we leave the scene. The police take the guy away.

*

A few days later, I see the same old guy back in the same area. He's eager to announce his presence to me.

"Yeah, I told you mother*cker. I'm unstoppable."

He doesn't live in the building. He just terrorizes the people who do.

"What are you doing here?" I ask.

"Man, I can do what the f*ck I want. I go where I want to go."

"You can't come around these buildings. I'm not going to tell you again."

"You ain't gonna' do sh*t!"

I grab him by the back of his neck and the seat of his pants. He spins in the air, screaming, and lands in nearby bushes.

He scrambles out. "Oh my god!" He takes off running.

*

The next day, I see the guy. He sees me, stops, and starts running. I give chase. I'm faster. I catch him and throw him in the bushes.

He's upset again. "Man, you can't just keep on throwin' me in the bushes!"

"Any time I see you in the neighborhood, you're going to be in the bushes."

"That's bullsh*t, man. That's bullsh*t."

"Well, it's bullsh*t you come around here terrorizing families and stab someone in the throat, and somehow you don't go to prison. So, here's what's going to happen to you when you come around here. You may not go to prison, but you will be going into these bushes."

He storms off.

*

A few days later, I'm driving with a couple of trainees in my organization. I see the guy about 100 yards away. He sees my car. He runs, and I start following. He zig-zags into an area he knows I can't drive the car.

I stop the car. "Get that guy."
The two trainees take off after him.

They're faster.

Standing against my vehicle, next to some bushes, I watch the trainees walk him back to me.

I look at him.

He speaks up. "I know y'all ain't gonna' throw me in them bushes."

The volunteers grab him by the collar and ankles. They swing him back and forth.

"Aw, hell nah!"

"One."

Swing.

"Two."
Swing.

"Three."

He screams as he flies into the bushes. He crawls back to his feet, yells in frustration, and runs off.

*

Twenty years later, I'm at a gas station three miles from where the man got stabbed. I see the guy that did the stabbing. Incredibly, he looks the same.

Is this guy a time traveler? A vampire?

He walks up to me while I'm standing at the pump.

"Hey, can I have a dollar?"

He doesn't seem to recognize me. "Hey, how you been doin'?"

"I'm fine, but I don't know you." He says this vehemently.

"You know me."

"No, I don't. I don't *know* you!"

"I'll give you five dollars if you do two things. Admit that you're you by shaking hands with me and to show that the past is the past and take a picture with me."

He thinks about it. "You'll give me five dollars?"

"Yes."
 He thinks about it more.

In a friendly tone, he says. "Man, how you been doin' man! Good to see you. After all these years!"

We shake hands. I take a picture.

***

In this story, I crossed a line I didn't want to cross.

The guy had stabbed someone. He tried to stab me. I had called the detectives for three days trying to get him prosecuted. The detectives refused to answer the phone, call me back, or charge the guy.

I believed in law and order. When law and order failed, I refused to fail. The system we have now is not set up to protect the people. I became a protector because I was a dedicated agent of change.

It's important to distinguish my actions from that of a vigilante. A vigilante is someone who seeks to dispense justice. I wouldn't let this guy walk around terrorizing and stabbing people in the community. I was doing what I had to do to keep people safe.

Characters played by Clint Eastwood, Chuck Norris, and Charles Bronson taught much harsher lessons. The eye-for-an-eye mentality that's paraded in front of us through fiction and movies is not effective in reality. Still, many people would believe I was within my rights to take things much further than familiarizing him with the local flora. He tried to stab me, and I gave him grass stains in return.

Chapter 20 Lessons

- Use code names to keep people from knowing who you are.
- Videos don't always tell an accurate story.
- Just because someone tried to kill you doesn't mean you have to kill them.

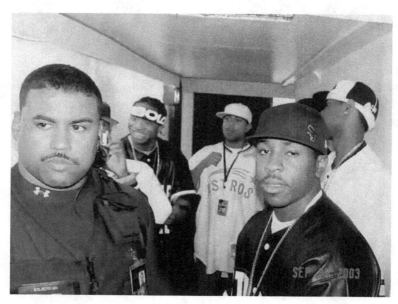

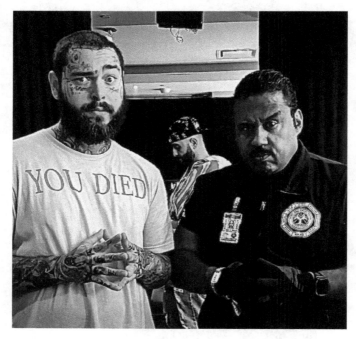

21

The Runners Who Walked Away

Detroit, Michigan

November 1997

1160 Holcomb

Approximately 4:00 pm

I receive a call that a drug dealer is harassing residents at 1160 Holcomb. I instruct the person on the other end of the line to call the police and that I'm on my way. I call the cops as well.

I arrive with two of my guys. They carry the code names Razor-16 and Talon-14.

A few individuals are milling around in the hallway, just inside the front door.

The alleged drug dealer is what I call a thug dealer. At this point, my organization has specific names for different types of individuals based on behaviors and motivations. Drug dealers are most interested in turning a profit. **Thugs are people who like violence for**

the sake of violence.

A thug dealer is someone who lies somewhere in between. They are violent people who deal drugs on the side.

This particular thug dealer would look like if Shabba Ranks and Flavor Flav had a baby. He's over 40, an inch or two taller than me, around 200 pounds, lean, kind of wiry.

I approach. "You need to leave."

Another individual walks through the front door. He's shorter, about 5'7 and around 150lbs. He's immaculately cut with a thin goatee. His build is athletic, and he has a darkness to him. He moves in very close to me. My hairs stand on end. He looks me in the eye. "You talkin' to me?"

This guy is serious.

I respond. "No, we're not talkin' to you."

"I thought you were talkin' to me." He continues.

"If I was talking to you, you would know because I would tell you."

"Oh, you sure?"

"I'm sure. I'm not talkin' to you. You have a good day."

He moves away and stands at the bottom of the stairs nearby. *This guy is weird.*

The thug dealer squares off to me. Our faces are inches from one another. "F*ck you. I'm not going. You can't stop me."

"You need to walk out on your own, or you'll be put out." We stare.

It's a staring match.

Razor-16 and Talon-14 are observing. They're trained by my organization. They've passed multiple tests to earn those code names. New recruits were referred to as candidates or Standard Auxiliary Units. 'S.A.U.' for short. The average person takes about 30 days to pass and earn their code name. 'Razor' was derived from the first letter of his first name, Ronny. '16' means he's my 16th employee with the letter "R" that successfully passed his training requirements.

The training is what I would call essential. It's procedural and tactical. Candidates have to prove they can disarm a gun, or a knife, know some laws to perform legally, and then there are some basic codes to be familiar with: code green, code blue, and code red. Basic defensive positions have to be learned. The exam is skill-based.

Talon-14 and Razor-16 are best friends. They look like a couple of actors. Tall, lean, and mean builds. They're popular with the ladies, and they get plenty of attention. Before they were part of my team, they were attacked by a group of six men with bats for racist reasons. Razor and Talon defended themselves and used the aggressor's bats against the attackers. The group fled and pressed charges. Razor and Talon were facing assault charges for protecting their own lives. Shortly afterward, they joined up with my organization.

The thug dealer starts backing towards the door. We press forward, and he steps outside. We move out with him and block the front door.

A third, very large, individual comes forward. He's approximately 6'6", 350 pounds, and aggressive.

He says, "What did you say to me?"

"We're talking to him." I indicate the thug dealer.

"Oh, I thought you talkin' to me. 'Cuz I'm out the street with yo lil' a**."

"Excuse me, sir? We're security for the building."

"No, I thought you talkin' to me."

"Sir, we're not talkin' to you." I repeat.

"No, what I'm sayin', if you talkin' to me, tellin' me I can't come in here, I'm out the street with yo a** right now."

"Sir, you're not going to do anything. In fact, because of your threats against security, we don't feel you're safe to go inside. Do not enter the building. It will be trespassing."

"Man, f*ck what you talkin' about. I told you I'm mop the street with yo a**."

"Sir, you're not going inside."

"Man, f*ck you!"

He heads straight for Razor-16. He's the size of an N.F.L. player, and he's charging like a professional lineman. Razor-16 looks like a singer Al B Sure he's also a champion wrestler. The two collide.

The dealer backs away.

Razor-16 pushes the bigger man's chin away and his elbow downwards. The charging giant spins around naturally. The Razor takes him to the ground fast and efficiently into a rear-naked choke. In three to five seconds, the giant lineman is rendered unconscious.

I'm impressed, but I'm worried. I wonder if one of my guys just killed someone. The big man isn't moving.

I began to have thoughts of fleeting, but Mexico is far away. I don't have enough gas to get there, and I don't speak Spanish.

Talon and Razor are on their feet watching. The big man is still as death.

Canada is too cold. I can't get stuck in Canada.

The giant starts to wiggle.

I start getting happy.

He comes to and climbs to his feet. "I'm callin' the po-lice!" He's upset, frantic, and half-crying. He takes off down the street. "I'm callin' the po-lice!"

The thug dealer speaks up. "Oh, I got somethin' for yo a**!" He takes off running towards a fuchsia, aka hot pink GMC Jimmy truck. By the looks of it, it has to be the only fuchsia jeep in America.

He hops in and starts the engine. I'm trying to read his plates. I call the police again. My guys and I move onto the street in front of the building. The jeep comes straight towards us.

All three of us leap out of the way. I'm still on the phone and will get a 911 operator to pick up. "There's a guy here attacking us. We're security—"

The jeep spins back around and rushes in again.

I yell at the operator, "He's coming back towards us now!"

The jeep accelerates down the street about one block. A police cruiser stops him near East Jefferson.

The police got here that fast? That's amazing!

As I head over to the cops, I see the thug dealer being handcuffed and put into the back of the squad car.

"Wow, that's fast. Thank you for being here so quickly." The officer responds.

"What do you mean?"

"You're responding to the guy trying to hit us with a car?"

"No, we just saw him speeding."

"Well, he was trying to hit us, trying to kill us. I'm a witness for attempted murder."

"OK, I'll write that down."

From the back seat, the thug dealer yells. "Oh, I got somethin' for you're a**."

"No, sir, you're about to go to prison. You tried to hit someone with a car." Irritated, I sigh.

"You gonna' see how it's done. I'll be right back." He continues.

"What do you mean?"

"I ain't goin' nowhere. I'll be right back. Believe me when I tell you I'll be right back."

"Sir, you tried to hit someone with a car. You understand? You tried to kill us. There's no way you're coming right back. Attempting to murder someone with a car is illegal. And you, sir, are going to *prison*. I guarantee that because I will be testifying."

"You ain't gonna' do sh*t. I'll be right back."

"Whatever." I'm done arguing with this thug dealer.

The police take my report and drive away with him in the back seat.

Approximately one and a half hours later, myself, Razor-16, and Talon 14 are standing in the parking lot in front of the building. The thug dealer comes back. His fuchsia jeep is parked where the cops pulled him over. He walks up to it, gets inside, and yells at us.

"I told you mother*ckers!"

*

The next day, at 1130 Holcomb, I'm in the parking lot when ten plain clothes officers rush into a nearby apartment building. Out front, I see a peculiar individual eating an ice cream cone. He looks familiar. He's the short guy eyeing us from the stairwell the day before. Once all of the officers are inside, he walks out of view.

A few minutes pass, and the officers exit the building. I approach and start a conversation with one of them.

He says, "We're lookin' for this guy, CJ Armstrong." He produces a picture. It's the guy I saw who was just out front eating an ice cream cone in plain daylight while the police rushed past.

"Oh, he was right out front when you guys went in. You literally ran right past him."

"Well, you need to watch this guy. He killed an entire family on the next block over. He's a drug hitman. He's wanted for killing multiple people and multiple families in multiple places on the East Side. He is a collector of debt for drug dealers."

That's why he was hanging around the thug dealer yesterday. The cop continues, "If you see him, let us know."

*

A few days later, I'm on patrol. Multiple women are telling me the same story of C.J. harassing them for sex. These women are terrified of this man who's planning to rape them. He won't take 'no' for an answer and has been trying to get into their apartments.

That night, it's cold but not snowing yet in Detroit. I'm walking my dog. He's grown up into a 100-pound brindle German Sheppard pit-bull mix.

While walking around East Jefferson, I see C.J. step out of a local bar. He's a friendly dog and not likely to bite anyone. But he looks the part.

I'm in tactical gear and armed. He sees me. I order him, "Don't move!" He looks at me.45 Caliber Pistol. "Don't shoot me."

I'm in a firing position.

He looks at the dog. "Don't let the dog go."

"I won't let the dog go, but don't run. If you start running, I'm gonna' let the dog go."

C.J. takes off running.

Dammit.

I give chase. We're running down the middle of East Jefferson. Cars are peeling off left and right.

Using my earpiece, I call the police. An operator picks up. Running and panting with gun and leash in hand, I speak up. "I'm security for the building. I'm running down the street chasing a wanted criminal. A murderer named CJ Armstrong."

The female operator doesn't sound impressed. "Well, stop chasing him."

"Ma'am, I can't stop chasing him."

"Stop chasing him, right now! You can't chase him!" She yells.

"Ma'am, send the police. He's wanted for murder. You have to send the police, right now."

"Stand by." She goes quiet.

C.J. is dusting me. I used to be a runner, but this guy is a hell of a sprinter. He's now about 150 yards in front and takes a left behind a gas station.

I go around the front and stop at a retaining wall. It's dark, and as I come to the edge of a 4-foot wall at the Shell gas station. I check to make sure I don't shadow cast. I don't want to give my position away.

C.J., somewhere in the shadows, yells out. "Don't follow me! I can see you!"

"Don't run. Stop where you are. Police are on the way!"

C.J. knows he cannot go to prison. If he does, without question, he is going away forever. We both know it.

"Don't follow me! I can see your dog's breath!"

I check my dog.

Dammit.

Sure enough, his panting is sending mist forward.

C.J. can see my location, but because of the 4-foot concrete wall, but he can't shoot me.

Nearby is an apartment building known as 'The Barracks.' It's relatively low rent, and a lot of police officers live there. C.J. is closer to The Barracks than I am. He's no more than 50 feet from me, but now I can't see him.

I hear feet shuffling. C.J.'s running. I take off in the direction of The Barracks.

"Don't follow me!" He yells.

The 911 operator comes back online. "What are you doing?"

"Now, I'm on McClellan and East Jefferson."

"What are you doing there?"

"I'm following the guy. Send the police. He's a murderer. He's harassing the women in our building. He's threatening the people. We need the police to pick him up. I have him here. I'm telling you where he's at. Come. Get. Him!"

"You need to stop right now. Stop following him, right now!"

Frustrated with the operator, I refocus on my surroundings and realize I'm exposed. Across from The Barracks is a grocery store. Between the buildings lies a football field of nothing. The Placard above my head reads "The Barracks." The field is pitch black, and I know the streetlights behind me have me back-lit. No doubt C.J. can see me in this position, though I still can't see him.

In total darkness, about 100 yards away, I hear C.J. "I told you, don't follow me!"

I hear gunshots. Within this range, in a city surrounded by high-rises, it sounds like I'm in a gun range.

The operator squawks in my earpiece. "Are you shooting?"

"No, he's pretty close." I state as I hide behind a high tree located in front of the Barracks.

But I can't pursue him. He has all the cover of darkness, and he's too fast. Not wanting to catch a bullet, I head home.

The walk is long, but I get back to my apartment. I head toward my security locker and put my gun and tactical gear away. All I have left on is a t-shirt that says 'U.S. Patrol' on it. Which stands for Urban Survival Patrol. I have on tiger-striped fatigue pants and magnum high tech boots. I'm still waiting for the police.

I wait and wait.

45 minutes later, the police show up. It's between 12:45 am and 1:00 am Six cops, one female and five males, come into the building. It's a tight 15 by 15 corridor, and they all have guns drawn.

I give a friendly smile. "Hey, I'm security. I'm Dale. I called you about a man with a gun, a few blocks from here, shooting at me, with a gun."

DETROIT URBAN SURVIVAL CHRONICLES

The cops are looking at me, but they're not responding. Their expressions are blank. Occasionally, they look at each other.

I try it again. "Hey, I'm security. I called."

No response.

"Hey, how's it going? Hello?" Their guns are still pointed at me. I'm more than a little concerned.

Another large officer walks in. He's a sergeant, has a beard, is about 6'3" and 300 pounds. "Alright, what's goin' on here?"

I speak up. "Hey, sarge. I called about the guy with the gun—"

The sergeant interrupts me, surveying his team. "Hey, guys, what are you doing? Put your guns away." The officers are still in their blank gun pointing trance.

The sergeant continues. "Put it away—ya know what. Everybody outside!"

I approach the sergeant outside. "It's CJ Armstrong. He's wanted for murder. 5th Precinct Special Ops Division was over here yesterday trying to get him. I'm sure you saw the picture."

"Nope."

I produce the picture.

"I don't know anything about this. What are you talking about?"

I'm baffled. *How can he not know?*

"The guy. Murderer. Murdered the families. Was over here. Raid team..."

"No, I don't know anything about what you're talkin' about."

"Really?"

Different divisions don't communicate? Cops don't share information about murderers.

I give a police report. The cops leave.

It's a bitter cold winter in Detroit, Michigan. Six inches of snow and ice blanket the city. My organization's new recruit is a young Jewish guy from the suburbs. He's a rich kid with a mature demeanor. He's 18, about to graduate high school, and to train with us. His father is an executive at Ford Motor. He likes to show videos to his buddies of himself working with an anti-terrorist organization in Detroit. Talk about bragging rights. He's a good kid, and he's not holding back.

We're in his truck, cruising around at night, when I see C.J. on the sidewalk. I can hardly believe it.

"Hey! That's him! That's CJ Armstrong! Pull up to him!"

The Ford truck pulls up, stops, and slides into the curb. I jump out onto the sidewalk. "Freeze! Don't move!"

C.J. stops. "OK, I'll stay right here. Don't shoot me."

"I won't shoot you if you don't move."

I'm on solid ice. I can barely stand and begin to slide to the left. C.J. notices and checks his footing. He's on the salted pavement. He glances at me and takes off running.

Dammit!

It's so slippery that I can barely get back to the truck, just a few feet uphill. By the time I do, C.J. is out of sight.

The kid and I head to the police station. We tell the cops C.J. is still around, and I make another report.

I was hoping he had finally left. For the last few weeks, my team and I have been doing 'gas checks' around the building C.J. stays in. He has some kind of deal with the manager, Keith. Keith looks and talks like Steve Harvey. People even call him Steve Harvey. He drives a BMW and is a church-going family man. He's educated with a degree in business finance. It's not unusual for apartment managers in Detroit to allow drug dealers to operate out of their buildings. Officially, the units the dealers stay in are 'vacant.' They keep the criminals off the books. In exchange, the managers get a cut of the drug money.

To avoid being busted by cops who obtain a search warrant, C.J. had multiple units. Each one was officially 'vacant' and had locks on the doors. When I brought it to the manager's attention, he acted surprised. "Can't believe these locks!" That was his plausible deniability. He avoided any direct contact with the drug dealers.

My strategy was to do gas checks, which meant kicking the doors. I thought C.J. might be inside. We'd find dope, money, and T.V.s all belonging to C.J.

If the unit was vacant, and I smelled gas, I was acting well within the law. For various reasons, gas smells permeated the entire building. My goal was to disrupt C.J.'s feelings of safety and motivate him to leave the building and the area. It pissed him off.

At around 4:00 pm, I finish the police report. I've dropped the kid off. I'm on Holcomb Street, heading towards East Jefferson. While driving, I see three masked guys approach a blue primer grey and blue car. It looks like it's being fixed up into a show car.

Haha, look at that. Looks so scary.

It's winter time. Lots of people wear masks to keep warm. My vehicle moves slowly, around 20 miles per hour. The men are about 25 yards away.

One of the men starts in my direction. It looks like he's running straight toward me.

He's not running toward me. That's bullsh*t. You need to calm down. You need to relax. You're being paranoid. That guy is not running towards you.

The man adopts a shooting position.

What? No. That's not going to happen. What is he doing?

Shots fire. I hear the low thuds of .45 caliber bullets under my seat. I lean to the right and accelerate. The barrels of my 4-barrel carburetor open wide. I have a straight pipe with a cherry bomb on dual exhausts. There's no muffler. It's deafening, and I'm accelerating on the icy street as fast as I can.

More shots ring out. Luckily, the shooter doesn't understand the trajectory. The bullets are skipping and bouncing under the bed of the car. I head straight back to the 7th Precinct as fast as I can.

Once there, I go in to make another report.

"Hi, I just left here. Remember? I just got shot at."

They send a blonde female of slight build, approximately 27 years old, to inspect my vehicle. She peeks under the car with a flashlight. After almost no time, she says, "I can't substantiate that there's bullet holes there because I can't see them."

I protest. "Ma'am, the fact that you can't see them doesn't change the fact that they're there."

"Well, I can't see them."

"I can't help you. I can't help you see them. I understand you can't see them. But that doesn't change the facts."

"Citizen I can't write it in my report. I'll write that you said it. But I can't write that it's substantiated."

Unbelievable.

I give up trying to persuade her to see bullet holes. "That's fine. It doesn't matter. Write whatever you want."

***

The blonde female police officer who refused to substantiate what she didn't see probably couldn't see the bullet holes. It was apparent at the time that she simply didn't believe me. She didn't believe there were any bullet holes to be seen. Cops are people. When we believe or disbelieve something, facts have little effect on our perception. Six months after she had not substantiated the bullet holes, I brought my vehicle in to a shop for maintenance. The mechanics opened things up a bit and called me over. They were aghast and showed me the bullet holes. They were clear as day. Large 45 caliber bullet holes, ripped wide open, sprawling metal.

The night I had chased C.J. in the dark, the police had taken an inordinately long time to show up. The reason was that one shift was ending while I was in pursuit. By the time he got away, the police were in complete shift change. Midnight was that time. That's why it took the police 45 minutes to an hour to show up finally. Their blank stares are what I have deemed the 'kill phase.' They showed up, believing that there was a dangerous shooter. They were not mentally present. Their brains were hyper-focused on any indication that now was a good time to start shooting. Only when the sergeant's voice boomed in their ears did they snap out of it. It's important to understand that our bodies undergo a shift in situations where guns are drawn and lives are at stake. Logical reasoning, listening, and most sounds do not register. Had I made a sudden movement or done anything registered as a threat, the police would have fired on me.

The sergeant's complete lack of knowledge regarding CJ Armstrong or my subsequent calls and reports was eye-opening. At the time, I was still figuring it out. Because of movies and commonly held beliefs, I assumed that different precincts within the same city communicated. I believed there were morning briefings and maybe a wall of known dangerous suspects in the areas. That's not the case. In reality, there is no widely familiarized list of top criminals within a city. Why the raid team did not register that C.J. was standing in front of them, I have no idea.

The thug dealer, who claimed he would be "right back" and then was, knew what he was doing. He was likely a criminal informant. After he showed back up, cussed us out, and zoomed off, I made a visit to the arresting officer. He was conservative, polite, and by the book. I was delighted to meet a professional cop. Ten years after that arrest, I saw him again. I said hi, and he explained what had happened. The thug dealer, once brought to the station, used his one phone call to contact Internal Affairs. He lied, stating that the police had robbed him of 700 dollars "all 20s and a five." For that, the arresting officer was taken off the street and put on desk duty for the next ten years. In my view, the cop distinguished himself as a stickler for the rules. That wouldn't be tolerated. How you get, mathematically, 700 dollars from all 20s and a five is a mystery to both of us.

From 1998 to 2012, I learned a lot about what I have control over and what I don't meaning some will get away. More than merely choosing my battles, I had to fully realize where my organization's niche was. U.S. Patrol, or Urban Survival Patrol, was not a popular name. My plan was to have an official-looking "U.S." stitched on our tactical uniforms that would suggest we were a branch of the government. Maybe people would think we were special forces of some kind. That was my plan, and it worked, sort of.

The name "VIPERS" found us, was applied and stuck, V.I.P.E.R.S., Which stands for Violence Intervention Protection Emergency Response System. There's nothing I can't make an acronym for. However, understanding our name will help you understand my actions regarding C.J. Unlike the little girl sprayed in the eyes, the one I could have protected but didn't, C.J. was not threatening anyone. V.I.P.E.R.S. are not law enforcement.

We are not "justice enforcement," either. We are violence prevention. If someone is doing something illegal but isn't physically harming anyone, we're not here to make an arrest or subdue someone for the police to apprehend. We are here solely for those whose lives are in danger. Criminals and law-abiding citizens who choose to be non-violent are not our priority. When it comes to violence, we do not compromise. We act rapidly and effectively. We neutralize threats. We focus only on de-escalating violent situations, never escalation in the name of the law or a perceived greater good. We create environments where violent behavior simply cannot thrive.

Chapter 21 Lessons

- It doesn't matter how big you are; you can still be taken down.
- A commanding presence goes a long way.
- Watch your shadow around corners (and your dog's breath).
- Beliefs dictate perception.
- Peace is better than prosecution.
- A life is more important than laws.

22

Cops, Cigarettes, and Job Interviews

Detroit Michigan

1998

I remember Eddie Murphy hanging out of the back of a truck in a sting operation on cigarette trucks. It seems so silly. Beverly Hills Cop is not reality.

It's just a movie.

Meanwhile, a group of middle eastern business owners is playing cards together.

One says to the others, "Hey, I'm having a problem with these hijackings, and all my insurance companies are canceling me. The police aren't able to stop them. The feds can't stop them. They are getting more and more out of control, and now I'm losing like 100 thousand a month from hijackings. All the insurance companies have terminated my contracts. I can't get insurance."

One business owner responds, "I know a group on the Eastside. They got rid of all of our gang problems that were robbing our grocery store. I can put you in touch with them."

"I appreciate that—these guys hi-jack more than one truck. My guys get hi-jacked, taken hostage, and in some cases even stabbed. We lost a million-dollar truck recently."

I get the call and end up sitting down with the owner of a 250-million-dollar cigarette company. He appears disinterested, but I make my pitch with confidence.

"We can protect the trucks. We can do whatever it takes to keep things safe. We work on the East Side of Detroit. We keep families safe. We keep businesses safe. We deal with gang members. The gangs don't mess with us. We can stop them."

"Really?"

"Yes, sir. We certainly can. We have no problems stopping gangs."

"OK, well, thanks for coming out."

When I head out, I think it didn't go so well. The business owner seemed underwhelmed. Even so, I'm happy to have had such an excellent opportunity for my organization.

I see a familiar face walking toward the building as I walk out. He's a bodybuilder and cop that I know. He looks like an African-American version of the HULK in Police uniform. In addition to being employed as a police officer, he runs an off-duty cop company that offers private protection services. He speaks first.

"Hey, what's up, VIPER! They're talking to you? They interviewed you?"

"Yeah, man, they're lookin' at hiring us. Ya know—"

"OK, I have to go in there now."

The cop makes his way to the table of the man I just interviewed. He says, before anything else, "Do you know who that was that just left your office?"

"Who? The guy who just left?"

"Yeah, you do know that's VIPERS, right?"

"OK—"

"Listen. Don't hire VIPERS. Those guys are barbarians. If you hire them, then you're going to get people hurt. That's why you hire VIPERS to hurt people. Never hire VIPERS unless you want people hurt."

"What? Wait. The guy who talks like Bryant Gumbel has barbarians? Really?"

"Yes. It's an army of them. They're known for being very violent."

"So—I can't imagine that. The guy who *just left here*, who talks like a sportscaster, has an army of very violent barbarians?"

"Yes."

"Well, I want to let you know that you just got that guy the job. I wasn't going to hire him because he talks so smart but, since you spoke up, I'm definitely going to hire that guy now."

"What do you mean? Why would you hire him? I have off-duty cops. We're all armed. We're all off-duty cops and military veterans. Why would you hire VIPERS?"

"Why would I hire you? I've been talking to police and sheriffs and state police and feds for ten years now. And the robberies just keep getting worse. All I hear is 'we're forming a task force. We're doing this; we're doing that.' Why would I hire you to do something off-duty that you can't do *on-duty?*"

"Well, um. That's not us."

"Yeah. That is you. That's the best of you. And they couldn't help me at all. So, you just got that guy the job."

I get a call. The business owner recites the whole conversation over the phone.

***

This story recounts the landing of a huge account for my organization. We've been successfully protecting this company and its trucks and drivers safe for 24 years now. Not in one of those 24 years has the company experienced a single fight, robbery, or lawsuit. That company is now a 300-million-dollar company because they had no hijackings.

In the beginning, the VIPERS worked out of nightclubs and small private companies. That was enough to sustain us, but we wanted to grow far beyond that. Once I landed a large account, I knew I couldn't apply the same nightclub tactics.

I created an internal threat management division for the cigarette company. The aim and achievement of this division were to create conditions where hijackings don't happen because hijackers don't think they can win.

My work started the day after the call. VIPERS and I brought in six vehicles with two men each. It wasn't difficult to ascertain that robberies occurred entirely within Detroit. So, we'd follow the cigarette trucks as they entered the city. We continued to follow them during all deliveries, all day, Monday through Saturday. Men, dogs, and vehicles were used to protect the trucks.

We currently follow these trucks, just not into Beverly Hills.

Chapter 22 Lessons
- Bad press, like in a job interview, can be good Super-rich business owners often lack verbal filters.

23
The Outcoaster Gang

Detroit, Michigan

November 1998

The River Rock Club

You can see Canada from the River Rock Club. We have been working here for a while without incident. This club makes a lot of money. It's the only club that is safe to visit.

The Outcoaster Gang is here tonight, as they frequently are. They're a biker gang, but we have what I would call a working relationship; no issues, and we co-exist.

Tonight, they're handing out fliers. It's their after-hours stripper-sex club. I see one of their higher-ups. He goes by Jokey and looks like an African-American version of Fidel Castro, green military cap and all. He's older, well into his 60's. Jokey is known as a hitman. The story is that he once walked into a gunfight between the Police and some thugs. The cops were pinned down. Jokey pulled out his 44-pistol and starts unloading on the criminals. He saves the cops, and an interesting new relationship forms.

The type of stripper-sex club they are advertising is known for having dead girls left in the dumpsters in the alleys behind them.

Lotus-11, a female team member, is from Mexico. She has a regal, traditional Mexican beauty to her. Her hair is done in a traditional royal style. She looks something like Salma Hayek with Princess Leia's hairdo. Lotus-11 handles herself at all times, very professional.

One of the women, a prostitute, and stripper that hangs around the Outcoasters, approaches. She looks albino, with blonde hair and blue eyes. Every VIPER in the club is aware that she's what the Outcoasters refer to as 'property.' The albino eyes Lotus-11 and starts talking. Lotus-11 in black tactical uniform stays reserved. The stripper begins touching Lotus-11 around her hips and reaches between her legs.

"Please don't touch me." Lotus-11 backs away and moves outside.

The albino female follows her outside. She's not giving up. She's touching her again.

Falcon-1, the team leader that night, notices what's happening. Falcon-1 is from Ann Arbor, like me. He looks like a soap opera star. He has light brown skin, green eyes, and light brown wavy hair. His unique appearance tends to attract female attention. He's professional, highly structured, and friendly, and he legally carries around an Squeeze-Cocking H&K P7 with him; an excellent firearm.

Falcon-1 approaches. "Hey sista, do you mind not touching our team member because she is just doing her job? So, if you wouldn't mind sista, could you please not touch her anymore?"

The stripper huffs and stomps off.

Falcon-1 shrugs.

Ten Outcoasters confront Falcon-1 in front of the River Rock Club approximately five minutes later.

"Did you just talk to our property? Don't no mother*cker talk to our property. Ever."

"Brother, we don't want any trouble. We don't ever have any problem with you guys out here. We work well with you out here. Your female property was touching our female team member."

"I don't give a f*ck what she was doin'. Don't no man talk to our property. You don't ever address our property."

"OK, no problem. In the future, can you just please have her do that?"

"F*ck you, you light-skinned mother*cker. We'll f*ck you up!"

Throughout the entire club, there are 26 VIPERS. Falcon-1 gives a signal. Ten VIPERS flank the ten Outcoasters and form a 'VIPER Wall.' The Outcoasters fan out. They're in a fighting position. The ten VIPERS are shoulder to shoulder in a 'ready position.' Their hands are clasped in the middle of their bodies. Legs are slightly apart, with the right leg forward and the left leg back. No VIPER speaks except the team leader.

Alpha-2 is the interior team leader. He steps forward, and everyone notices. He's Canadian, 6'9", and 380 pounds. He looks like Stone

Cold Steve Austin on steroids. He starts shaking a canister of pepper spray.

An Outcoaster speaks up in a hostile tone. "Hey. Whatcha' goin' do with that motherf*cka?"

"Commander Brown says I have to warn you. And I'm not supposed to do anything before I spray. So, I'm getting ready to spray you if you continue to aggress. As I was instructed by protocol by Commander Brown."

"F*ck you and your commander, mother*cker. We gonna' f*ck you up!" The Outcoasters move forward.

Alpha-2 sprays all ten of them in the face and eyes with a 10-percent pepper spray fogger. He's spraying two and three at a time very efficiently.

The VIPERS back up to avoid the fumes.

Jokey moves in to assist. He gets sprayed, too.

The Outcoasters are on the ground rolling and screaming.

The VIPERS tell them to stand down and attempt to escort them to a fence by voice. "OK, move to your left..."

We bring them water to rinse their eyes. Once they regain their sight, they leave.

*

The next night, I get a call from the owner of the River Rock Club. He's from Pakistan and is freaking out. 50 Outcoasters on Harley-Davidson motorcycles have just shown up.

With me is M-27. He's a country guy who uses a 9mm rifle to take down deer with headshots at 100 yards. He's a fantastic shooter and is our counter-sniper. He's in the adjacent building covering me.

I call the Police, and they enter the scene. There are seventy bikers, four cops, and fifteen VIPERS, including myself and M-27. Twenty more Outcoasters on foot show up.

I recognize one of the officers and approach. This cop's head is shaped like a peanut. He's 25-30 years old and is the typical Detroit cop. He's known affectionately as Peanut-Head, by Police and the public.

"Hey, watch these guys. I'm pretty sure quite a few are armed."

Peanut-Head scoffs. "Man, we got this. You wait here." He approaches the Outcoasters.

"Man, these mother*ckers attacked us yesterday. They sprayed us. And we here to do what we gotta do."

"Yeah, we understand." Peanut-Head then turns towards me. "Why did y'all do that to them?"

Is he complaining for the gang?

"Because they were goin' to attack our guys. Our guys were being nice."

Peanut-Head continues, "What do you mean being nice?"

"If we spray them, their teeth stay in their mouth. Their blood stays in their body. Their skulls are not impacted. We train three hours a day. There's no way they would not be seriously injured if things got physical. They don't know how to fight."

No one speaks.

"There's no way they could have a ballistic battle because I'm ten steps ahead on that, too. Ultimately, the pepper spray fogger did them a favor." I continue.

Jokey steps forward. "Man, I got the cataracts. Ya man sprayed. That white boy sprayed me!"

"First of all, he did exactly what he's supposed to do. He's Canadian. He is the team leader of the floor. He came out because your team members threatened us after sexually assaulting our female team member. They're supposed to come out and protect. That's exactly what they did. They're at work, man. These people have families. They're protecting the people inside. We're at work; we're not a gang. You guys do something else. These guys are actually physically working to support themselves and their families. They have to protect themselves, and others."

Jokey doesn't look satisfied. "Yeah, but they sprayed me! He was laughing, too. Yo white boy was laughing."

"OK, he was laughing. I believe you. That's because it's funny. It is funny, you have to admit, ya know, people are attacking, and they're not attacking, and ya know—usually, when people are violent towards us, we beat them down. And ya know, there's blood every-where, and they're seriously hurt and have to be carried away. Now, because we're doing things differently, we're using pepper spray, m'kay? Because we don't want to hurt people. We don't want to see people bleeding, broken bones, broken jaws, broken eye sockets, teeth missing—we found a way to use chemicals instead of our knees, elbows, fists, batons, everything else we have. We found a way to create less injury."

More silence.

They're listening.

"Think about this. If that team member, Alpha-2, at 6'9" 380 pounds, would have used his tactics, do you know your guys in your group would be seriously happy? Their eyes wouldn't be burning and then fine the next day. Their jaws would be broken. That's what happens when people fight. Their teeth are missing. They're bleed-ing. That's not what happened to your guys. You came to attack us, and everybody was brought to a safe condition without bleeding."
"Man, that's bullsh*t. My eyes still hurt right now."

I'm looking and talking directly to Jokey at this point. "I understand. I apologize it had to happen. You have to admit that this is better than the alternative, right? And you know that's how we win, that's how we succeed. We dominate threats. When violent people come to attack us, we always win. Over all these years. You know that."

Jokey turns abruptly and storms off. All at once, the 50 Outcoasters jump on their bikes and rumble off in formation. The 20 on foot leave, too.

*

The next day I'm at my school. A man on a Harley pulls up and steps inside. I approach him, and he says 'hi.' He's 60 years of age. He looks like a businessman that lifts weights. He's a very strong-looking African-American male with a goatee.

"Do you know who I am?"

I respond that I don't.

He's looking around with a smile. "You have a fine organization here. You're doing good things for the community. That's good. I heard good things. I really admire that."

We chat a bit more, but he doesn't have much else to say. As he leaves, I see some team members pulling up. When they enter, a couple of them have concerned looks on their faces.

"Commander Brown, do you know who that is?"

"No." I said.

"His name is Dark Night. He's the head of the Outcoasters."

***

This story may seem to violate a past chapter lesson. How do 15 men show superior force against 70?

The Outcoasters are a national organization. The 20 on foot were younger. Every one of the men on Harley's was huge and middle-aged. There is a clear structure, and every member has to earn their wheels. They earn a higher rank by procuring illegal things like women, girls, guns, drugs, and stolen motorcycles. Only 1 percent of the Outcoasters have bikes, and the gang is entirely African-American. For a woman to be considered 'property,' she is required to have sex with any of the members whenever they choose. The Outcoasters also offer security, albeit very differently than the VIPERS do. They are more like hired-muscle to defend against or take down the competition. The Outcoasters are known in Detroit for being very violent.

The nightclub owners were making between $30,000 and $50,000 per night. That was entirely off-the-door fees and drinks. The place was packed every night because it was one of the only safest clubs in the city at the time. That's all thanks to us, by the way. The owners used the profits to build palaces in Pakistan.

Jokey was one of the top guys of the Outcoasters and may still be. He's the guy they call to hunt down and kill people. His ability is what gives him a lot of influence within the organization. You don't get to be alive at his age by being bad at your job. It was Jokey that everything hinged on. He could have easily signaled an attack, and he was the one who called everything off. When I was speaking to him in front of Peanut-Head, Jokey's job was to assess the threat. I convinced him that if he attacked us that he couldn't survive.

Chapter 23 Lessons

- The group that is better trained and better organized has the advantage.
- Pepper spray is a powerful neutralizing agent.
- To de-escalate threats, the perception of superior force is more important than actual superiority.

24
Mantis-28 and the Candy Factory

Detroit, Michigan

A 17-year-old kid starts work at a candy factory straight out of high school. It's a family-owned business.

The kid does well in his role. Now in his 30's, he's making six figures.

The factory has been in business for about 40 years. They are a 20-million-dollar family-owned potato chip company that delivers all over the United States, Mexico, and Canada.

The 30-year-old manager has been there long enough that he decides to run a scam. He creates a fake worker on the shifts he runs. The guy then pockets the nonexistent worker's check, bringing his salary to nearly 200 thousand dollars annually. He cashes the checks at a liquor store, and that's how the owner finds out about it.

The owner decides to fire the shift manager for embezzlement. He's not interested in pressing charges. He just wants the guy gone. The shift manager responds, "Well, you can't fire me."

"Uh, yes. We're going to fire you."

Conversation ends. The guy gets fired. The owner hires a replacement.

The next day, the previous shift manager wraps his hand in a towel as a show of threat. He begins driving around the factory, threatening to kill everyone, including the newly hired manager.

"I'm going to kill you. I'm going to shoot you and kill your family."

The new manager quits, and another gets hired.

The same threats reoccur, and the second replacement hire quits.

It goes on this way. New hires come and go. The Police get called, they come to look for him, and they never catch him in the act or see him near the business. The video surveillance shows different cars, and it does not show the occupants inside the cars.

The license plates are removed or fictitious.

The owner is expanding to hiring out of state. They relocate the new manager to Detroit, where he is promptly hunted, chased, and scared off. He quits. Five managers so far.

The factory next hires a female manager. She's relocated from out-of-state. Her entire family moves to Michigan.

The old manager terrorizes her. She quits.

The Police tell him there is nothing they can do. However, they will keep trying. Frustrated, the factory owner is desperate. He has no idea what to do. A police officer refers him to our organization, and he calls us!

I drive into the factory. It's an enormous, sprawling complex in a rough part of town. I'm driving around for observation. I see the ex-manager here and there. He's using different vehicles.

One day, VIPERS and I recognize him behind the wheel of an un-familiar car. We nearly trap him and his vehicle within some fencing, but he blows past us.

VIPERS sit on the building, scaring him off when they can. The female manager restarts the position.

While protecting the area, we get reports of suspicious activity. A group of guys who look like they're part of the Duck Dynasty cast, big, rough, and very out of place in inner-city Detroit, hang out with a big brown van.

VIPERS pull up, blocking the van in. They ask some questions while noticing crates being loaded into the van.

We call the Police. The trailer park crew is arrested and prosecuted for stealing products.

Potato chips packaged to go to Mexico and Canada are showing up in neighborhood markets in Detroit. The owner is aware but doesn't understand why.

VIPERS and I, at this point, have worked in the factory for about a month. A report on us is done, and we get a call from the COO.

"We'd like to talk to you because all we can tell you is that we have some other problems here. We don't know what's going on. Our potato chips are in the wrong areas, in different countries. Do you have a plan that could help us?"

I select an infiltrator, Mantis-28. He's a giant. He's violent. He has a lazy eye, a comedian, and he's very popular and lucky with the ladies. I approach.

"Hey, I have a job for you. You're going to be undercover as a new manager in training. And you're going to find out what's going on for one week."

He's receptive.

One week goes by. I get a call from Mantis-28.

"Oh my God. So much stuff."

He briefs me:

The manager who got fired was a major drug dealer on the west side of Detroit. He owned about ten houses, 30 cars, and some used car lots. He was in charge of hiring people for the shift and in doing so, was supposed to screen people for criminal history through temp agencies. Instead, he *only* hired criminals with backgrounds in violence and robbery. The ex-manager stacked every shift with criminals. He was selling drugs, loan sharking, and women (prostitutes he hired as shift workers) to 150 people throughout the factory, every shift.

The day after the one-week Mantis-28 worked, VIPERS, Mantis-28, and I walk through the factory in full tactical VIPER uniforms.

The day after that, the loading docks, truck loading, and truck dispersal managers quit without notice. Each of them held a six-figure per year position.

My organization gets paid well for our work. Then we get a call from the factory owner a month later.

"We don't know what happened, but we want to make you guys a permanent part of our company. Our productivity went up 30% since you guys did our walkthrough. We want to set up a threat management division within our company".

I re-insert Mantis-28 as the head of the threat management division for the company. My cut is one thousand dollars per week, and so is Mantis's.

He goes to the COO directly after Mantis-28 has the new job.

"I can work for you directly without working for Commander Brown."

The COO responds, "Oh, OK, that'll save us a thousand dollars a week. I'll cut Commander Brown out of the deal."

I have two-way pagers called TimePorts. They're mine, I own them, but I loan them to VIPERS to keep track of everything that is said and done.

I approach one of the VIPERS that was close to Mantis-28.

"Give me the Time Port."

"What?"

"Give me the Time Port, which I own, and let you use for work."

I check the messages.

One from Mantis-28 reads:

"Check this out. This is the deal they offered. $1000 a week, 40 hours a week, and I call the hours randomly 24 hours a day, seven days a week, and I get an office."

I make a call to the CEO. They fire Mantis-28.

Five years later, the COO of the factory calls me.

"Ya know what. Your organization is the best protective organization I've ever seen. We've had some other issues. We've had to deal with Police on some things. We had some other company we dealt with. Honestly, nothing comes close to you guys. I'm working on a separate project for a separate company. It's a hospital strike. They need protection right now for the doctors coming into the hospital. How much do you charge for that?"

"$10,000 a day for ten guys."

"OK, I will get back to you."

The strike gets settled without our intervention.

I later discovered that Mantis-28 has been working for the city of Detroit since 2001. He drives books around for the school system. He still does, as far as I can ascertain.

****

This story reveals a diabolical scheme to turn an entire factory into an organized criminal operation under the noses of the chief officers. I was proud to be able to troubleshoot and apply highly effective measures to help the company get through such a big problem. However, it works more as a lesson in betrayal in business.

I learned that you could not trust people to do what's in their best interest. People are self-destructive by nature, as in Mantis-28's case. I gave him an incredible opportunity that he swiftly squandered.

In addition, I learned the importance of evaluating people based on who they show themselves to be.

Chapter 24 Lessons

- In business, have tight contracts.
- It is not uncommon for people to bite the hand that feeds them.
- Doing business at a high level can often mean war and betrayal within the organization.

25
Madame and Murderer

Windsor, Ontario

July 1998

A man calls, and he says he's the boyfriend of a woman who is in trouble.

The leader of Hell's Angels is hunting her in Canada. He's also her ex-husband.

The boyfriend is a gambler and wants to employ me and VIPERS as bodyguards.

"Can you help her?"

"Yes, we can."

People regularly cross the border to Ontario, Canada, it's not a big deal, but we're there to work. We don't have work visas. We meet her at a casino.

The Royal Canadian Mounted Police, RCMP for short, is at the casino with her. These guys are the Canadian equivalent of the FBI in the US, and they're asking her to testify against her husband, who's being charged with mass murder over ten separate killings. However, they don't like that we don't have work visas.

"They can't work here. No visas."

Alpha-2 is with me. He's Canadian, is 6'9", and 380 pounds. He's not allowed in any public social area in Canada. No nightclubs. No bars. This is because he kept getting into fights. He likes to fight, but he's very disciplined—even soldier-like around me. The RCMP recognizes him.

"How ya doin' Adam?"

"Fine, sir."

Another one of the VIPERS, 112-Jag, is with us. He's 19 but passes for 25 with a mature demeanor. He's built like a football player, short, wide, very intelligent, and a good fighter.

The woman resembles Dolly Parton, only thinner. She's educated, and professional, and is the owner of two brothels that employ over 50 girls, legally, in Canada.

She responds. The RCMP allows us to protect her in exchange for her testimony. "I don't trust any of you, but I trust these Americans. If you don't let them do their job, I'm not going to testify. Period."

We get to work that day. We escort her to her home. The Windsor, Ontario SWAT team has quarantined the entire block off. Black Suburban sit on either end and along the street. Machine guns are mounted on top.

Myself, Alpha-2, and 112-Jag, and a few other members of my organization surround the woman, our client, as she walks into her house to gather her things. She's planning to stay in the casino until she finishes her testimony.

VIPERS and I are with her twenty-four hours a day, seven days a week.

At the casino, we stay in an adjoining room.

We escort her to and from the courthouse. She testifies. Her ex-husband goes to prison.

***

I learned a few things about my foreign neighbors up north in the events above. I felt terrible for the brothel owner. The RCMP had tapped her ex-husband's phone. They recorded him, stating that he would kill her because she knew too much. She knew where the bodies were buried. They used the recording to flip her. She was terrified.

The cops offered protection but said it wouldn't be twenty-four hours a day.

The head of the biker gang had to make her disappear, or he would go to prison and never get out. He's currently in prison or dead. If not for my organization, I'm confident this woman would not be alive today. The Canadian authorities had a plan to protect her, but no one to implement the actual protection.

Chapter 25 Lessons

- The protection of life is more important than the enforcement of laws.
- The RCMP decided that the witness's testimony was more important than any law.
- The public and the Police need to work together to create the safety required to protect crime witnesses and victims.

26
Arizona Abduction

Detroit, Michigan

November 2012

I receive a call from a Detroit Police Department, domestic violence victim advocate. There's a young lady who needs help. She's being held in the shelter. She has no ID or anything else on her. But she does have an attorney to speak up for her.

A few VIPERS and I conduct our due diligence by investigating what the attorney tells us. We dig up and review documents like Personal Protection Orders (PPOs), witness statements, and hospitalization records. Many of these documents are provided by the lawyer, who is a certified officer of the court.

I can act legally based on documents produced and validated by such an officer.

The victim and her attorney came to our facility for assistance. She's Hispanic, about five feet tall, and approximately 100 pounds. She's crying. I can tell she's been distraught for days, weeks, or months.

Her 2-year-old daughter has been abducted by her father, who is also her husband. She's terrified of him.

I give the husband, who has the kid, a call.

"Hey, sir. We're with Threat Management Center. We have to verify the health and wellness of the child."

"I don't want any of that. This is my child. You understand me—" He goes on at some length.

We go back and forth. Eventually, I get him to drop his defense.

"I understand. We just have to make sure the child is OK. We're volunteers, making sure everything is fine."

"OK."

Two black Crown Victoria's with dark tinted windows pull up to his home, along with my Hummer. On the back of my H2 is the phone number for my organization.

111 Mantis, a VIPER, and my wife step out of the Hummer with me. We walk to the front door, and he opens the door and lets us in.

He's eager to keep things cordial and get this over with. "I'll show you the child's OK."

"OK, great."

We see the child and say she looks fine. We walk to the doorway near the kitchen. He walks into the kitchen. The mother, a domestic violence victim, walks into the house. 111 Mantis walks behind her as he proceeds to the child's room. The mother picks up her daughter, and 111 Mantis escorts her out of the house.

The husband reacts. "Hey, she can't be in here!"

"Yes, sir, this is her house. It's on her identification. She can be in here. You can't stop her from being in her own house. It's on her ID."

"But she can't take my child!"

"Sir, it's her child too, right? She can do whatever she wants. But you can't touch her. We will protect her. We're not touching the child, but you can't touch her."

"Oh—" He gets it and can't do anything at this point.

We escort the woman and her child to the airport. She flies out of Michigan to her home in Arizona, where the child was abducted from.

Once we see her off, we hop back into the vehicles. It's a happy moment.

One of the VIPERS, an ex-pro baseball player named Brian Johnson, speaks up, elated. "That was the greatest thing in the world to see the mother reunited with her child. A great rush."

He has three world series rings, and he's blown away by helping this woman.

On the way back, I get another call. The voice on the other end of the line identifies himself as a Federal Agent.

"Who are you guys? We just saw you pull up and go inside the house. What was that all about?"

I explain. We chat a bit. He got my phone number off the back of my truck.

He asks a few more questions. "How do you know she's telling the truth?"

"We spoke with the lawyer who represented the woman and validated the information via Police and medical reports. And, on top of all what the husband did, his brother is a drug dealer who's in prison right now."

"We know. We have the husband under surveillance right now for dealing drugs. I personally put his brother in prison last year."

After our chat, I hang up.

The phone rings. It's the Detroit Police. A woman speaks, but she's not drilling for answers. She has information for us.

"Off the record, we think you guys are good guys. But we just got contacted by Channel 2 News. They're about to do a story about a para-military group infiltrating and abducting a child. This is off the record, but why are they saying you guys abducted a child?" "If you want to tell us you can, but you don't have to."

DETROIT URBAN SURVIVAL CHRONICLES

I give her the story. She's receptive but can't do anything to set things straight with Channel 2 News.

I reunited a woman with her child after the kid was abducted by a drug dealer to be sold to a buyer in Yemen, and now I'm going to be put on TV for infiltrating and abducting the kid.

I get a hold of a contact in the mayor's office who deals with the media regularly. He knows the reporter planning to run the story about me abducting a child.

I call her. She gives me a chance to clear my name.

"OK, what happened?"

I fill in all the details.

"You can prove that?

"Yes, ma'am, we have all the video."

She goes through it all. She meets up with my team and me at our facility. I produce the video footage.

"Wow. I'm glad you caught me. This is our best story!"

I'm more than relieved, and later on, I watch myself on TV as the hero instead of a child abductor.

***

This story shows how crime and law are at once complex and straightforward.

227

The complexity comes from the web of communication, officers, and authority figures surrounding the issue. PPOs, witness statements, various credentials, media reporters, mayor's office liaisons, federal agents, Police, and then there's the woman's story itself.

The woman in question was approximately 25 years of age. The husband, about 35 years old, married her a year ago. He was originally from Yemen and was what you'd call a prescription drug dealer. He had put the house in her name to protect his criminal enterprise, so he had no actual claim to the house. His family was wealthy and owned multiple storefronts. The woman assumed that the money he brought came from his wealthy parents. It wasn't. He had hidden his drug dealings from her entirely.

His brother had been put in prison, and he needed money. He sold, as is not uncommon, his two-year-old child to a buyer in Yemen as a means to get the buyer a United States Passport. In exchange, the husband received 100,000 dollars.

Once the mother learned about who her husband was and that her child had been sold, she fled with the baby to Arizona. She holed up there away from her husband for months. He pleaded with her over the phone that he had changed, that he wasn't the drug-dealing baby-selling abusive man he once was. He begged her to allow him to see his child. Eventually, she caved. She made an effort to make the past the past, to not proceed as a married couple, but to allow him to see and spend time with his daughter.

The husband drove from Michigan to Arizona in a brand-new white Cadillac Escalade. The plan was that he would take his wife and baby out to eat. They ate as a family and returned to the vehicle. She secured the baby in the back seat while he got into the driver's seat.

Before she could enter the passenger seat, he locked the door and took off back to Michigan.

Getting the kid back was straightforward in verifying information and looking at what we, as an organization, could and could not do legally. Once we understand the boundaries, the way to the resolution makes itself apparent.

Chapter 26 Lessons

- Parents selling their children internationally is real.
- Non-violent resolution is at once complex and simple.
- You never know who is watching you or what their story will be.

27
Stalker Licks Mirror

Detroit, Michigan

July 2003

A woman working as a real estate agent and cosmetologist meet a guy at a party. He seems interested in finding a property, so she hands out her card. Some time passes, and he wants to buy a house but cannot be approved.

He asks her for help.

She says, "Well, I can't help you."

He says he wants to be in a relationship with her.

"I have a boyfriend."

Some time passes, and she receives cards containing money from the guy. She doesn't touch the cash and keeps everything in the envelopes. He's still calling her, hitting on her. She rejects him further, "I'm not interested."

"Well, you're my wife. You're going to be my wife."

The woman gets the Police involved. The man says it's a lover's spat. The woman says she's never dated him; they aren't together. The cops don't know who to believe.

The prosecutor's office in Oakland County, Michigan, refers the stalking victim to my organization for assistance. The prosecutor fills me in on the details and verifies the victim's statements and the need for protection.

The prosecutor states, "Wow, it's great that you're helping to protect this lady."

I then informed the prosecutor, Lisa Gorcyca, who's now a Judge, that I am the one who found the payphone he was calling from and saw him pull up to her business, and I scared him away. The stalker licked the window of her car, then licked a mirror inside her apartment. He had bought keys from the maintenance worker of the apartment building she lived in, in the suburbs of a city called Southfield. He got into the house and was licking the mirrors in her house. She has two young daughters."

The VIPERS volunteer to protect the stalking victim and escort her to church, to events and escort her kids to school. Eventually, she gets the guy on a recording.

"Why are you doing this to me?"

"Cuz we're supposed to be together. I love you."

"But we're not together. We never were together. I've never dated you. Why would you think we would be together if I've never ever been on a date with you?"

"Cuz. Cuz you know I love you—" and he continues on a diatribe about being together and raising her children.

"You can't raise my kids because we're not in a relationship."

The guy is arrested, found guilty, and sent to prison. In the courtroom, he's not happy.

"I'm going to sue her. I'm going to sue the Threat Management Center, sue the Police, sue the FBI, everybody, for millions of dollars for wrongful convictions."

A couple of years go by, and my organization receives our first award in 2005 for helping domestic violence victims for free in Oakland County.

In 2013 Channel 4, Channel 2, Investigation ID, and True TV all pick up the story. I'd flown to New York City to be on a TV show with the woman.

***

The stalking victim's sister was a police sergeant. The guy was sinister enough to call the Police ahead of time and claim that her sister was using her police powers to harass him. The sergeant's sister got in trouble, even though she hadn't done anything. The stalking victim got a personal protection order (PPO) early, which the man violated multiple times by trying to come into physical contact with her. The man had made an interesting case against Threat Management Center in court.

"Your honor, she hired Taliban. Those guys (VIPERS) are Taliban. I went to their website. They got rocket launchers."

The event allowed my organization to connect with a critical county prosecutor's office and a prosecutor who later became a judge.

Chapter 27 Lessons:

- Cunning criminals can manipulate the legal system.
- Harvest Williams did the right thing by collecting all the evidence required to prove she was being stalked relentlessly for years.
- Harvest Williams courageously created a non-profit organization called Michigan Coalition Against Stalking. She created the Stalkers Registry, where people like her stalker can be documented by their victims to prevent stalking others.

28
A Divorced Banana

Detroit Michigan

March 2004

The Oakland County prosecutor's office calls me. It's the victim's advocate.

"We need your help with this victim. We would like you to help her if you can."

They bring me in, and I meet the woman. She's European-American, approximately 55 years of age. Her jaw is wired shut. She has about 20 stitches in her forehead where her skull had been cracked open. She can still kind of talk.

"I went to the grocery store out in the suburbs, and a black guy came up and attacked me and did this to my face."

The suburb she's referring to is an area that has no significant African-American presence there. Any African-American male that so much as walked through the area had a high probability to be stopped and harassed by the Police.

Oh, wow. OK.

She goes on a bit more, and I follow up with the prosecutors. The attack was said to happen in broad daylight.

Yeah, it probably didn't happen. But, if I say that. The prosecutors will probably get mad, so I approach with caution.

"Is she OK?"

"Yeah, she's fine. She's a great person. We love her. We adopted her. We think she's a great person. She's having problems with her husband."

The woman has ten children. Her husband is a prominent Surgeon. They're very wealthy, and he wants a divorce. She's very depressed. I go to her for more details.

"The black guy who did this to my face and broke my jaw and broke my face, I saw that same black guy talking to my husband before."

OK, umm. She's lying. I can solve this problem right now.

I ask the advocate, "Have we vetted this story because I don't think— did you look at the cameras at the grocery store?"

"Oh, it's off-camera where she parked."

"And what was she doing at the grocery store?" I asked.

"She was buying a banana."

Did she go to buy one banana at a grocery store? She parked off-camera in the only parking space not covered by a camera. A black guy talking to her husband who wants to divorce her has now broken her skull and left. He didn't rape her, take her, or rob her. He just broke her face open with her car door and left.

"Here's the thing. I think there's something wrong with the story. She's probably depressed about the fact that her husband wants to divorce her, and I think we should look at that."

The prosecutor and the advocate lash out. "Why can you not believe her? She's so sweet. We're adopting her as a member of our family. We love her. We think this is real and this is true. We need your help if you can help her."

"Just in case, let's look at some counseling for her, maybe." I said.

"No! She is one of the smartest women I know. She's a great mother. She has ten children."

If I don't agree to help them with this craziness—I won't expand past Detroit. This is a chance for my organization to break out of Detroit and be an asset to the legal community of the state's wealthiest and most influential county. This is my chance to link with them. Or do I tell the truth, but then I know the truth will piss them off, and be put out of this office.

"Oh, I'm sorry, I see your point. Yeah, she's a good person. We'll put up a camera outside her house. Are there any witnesses, by the way?"

"No, there's no witnesses. We interviewed the Police, and they interviewed the people out there. They can't find anything."

"The Police are going to put up a cellular camera, and we'll go from there."

A few days pass. The camera yields nothing. She calls the cops.

"He's coming to the house! He's coming to the house! It's the same black guy. The black guy just came to my door!"

The Police have proof that she's lying. The prosecutor and victim's advocate find out she's lying.

She's prosecuted and goes to prison.

****

The woman deceived the prosecutor and victim's advocate and took advantage of their trust and generosity. Unfortunately, in my opinion, she was adversely affected by mental trauma.

Her husband was a prominent surgeon. He wanted a divorce. Further investigation showed that the man's children weren't allowed toys their entire life. The house was to be kept in perfect clean order at all times. This type of strict behavior takes a toll on a family. Once he decided to divorce the woman, she lost her mind. She needed mental care and assistance.

The prosecutor's office prosecuted her.

No man was attacking her off-camera when she went to buy a banana. Case closed.

Chapter 29 Lessons

- It is better to be kind then honest in many cases.
- Do not believe people just because they want you to.
- Understanding what someone's going through is necessary to helping their situation.

29
Motors and Men: The NOLA-Katrina Mission

Part 1

Detroit, Michigan

September 2005

What happened in New Orleans in September of 2005 was felt throughout the country.

In early September, Shepard Smith of Fox News seems to be the only prominent news network reporter showing coverage. The scenes are horrific.

One of my V.I.P.E.R.S. Team members, 100 Jag, comes to me about the people of New Orleans needing supplies. "We should help those people."

I'm proud of him. 100 Jag has blonde hair and looks like a skinhead. He's had minimal contact with African-Americans throughout his life, yet that doesn't stop him from volunteering to risk his life for people of a different ethnic group on the other side of the country. Also, I agree the victims of hurricane Katrina lack basic necessities like food and water.

However, the situation is hazardous. Gangs are out of control, people are dying, and there's little-to-no assistance as the flood cut off logistical support for the people in New Orleans. I asked my teammates to volunteer to help the families in need.

A team of volunteers is formed.

We reach out to our network to ask for financial assistance with the mission. My client is the only person willing to donate financial assistance; she donated 3,000 dollars. This money would only be used for logistical critical mission needs. The Detroit boat club gives us two flat-bottom Jon-boats. Hans, a competitive rowing instructor for an all-girls competitive rowing team that used the dilapidated Detroit Boat Club boat storage and training area, joins our team. He teaches me how to operate the small Jon-boats without motors; he looks and talks like Bryant Gumbel.

The five of us, a van, two boats, and my Hummer, drive straight through to New Orleans in 24 hours. I bring my dog, too. His name is She-Jin. He's a 150-pound Brazilian Mastiff. The breed was designed for hunting down and killing humans. He was trained to be a protector, and he was a sweet dog. He loved smiling at people.

The team has three V.I.P.E.R.S. and two other volunteers. Greg, the bulldog Mattics, a Kronk boxer a.k.a. Gamma-14, is one of them. He's an executive director of a non-profit program in downtown Detroit. He's also a Kronk boxer who was going pro at one point.

Two guys are in the 15-passenger van full of medical supplies. The other three, including myself, are in my H2. I've got a fake camera mounted on top, but it looks horrifying.

We enter Louisiana, and cell service becomes spotty as we get closer to New Orleans. Once we get into St. Bernard Parish, our G.P.S. cuts out.

Every few miles, there's a checkpoint. I make 100 Jag drive. He looks the part. They ask who we are.

"Detroit Threat Management," he says in a matter-of-fact tone.

We're wearing tactical gear with I.D. tags. They wave us through each checkpoint. I'm FEMA-trained, but I'm surprised we're not being turned away as we go.

Getting closer to the city, we see signs of devastation. Debris, broken trees, and large boats litter the highway landscape miles from the water, and torn billboards mark the sides of the highway. I get the feeling we're entering a zombie apocalypse movie.

100 Jag, who looks like an Aryan Nation Leader, continues to do well as our first point of contact.

In St. Bernard Parish, the men at the checkpoints are national guards.

Martial law is in effect, and no one is allowed in.

They question us, "Who are you with?"

"Detroit Threat Management."

It works again. They wave us on.

I see a military helicopter fly overhead. A battleship can be seen on the horizon from St. Bernard Parish. The U.S.S. Tortuga, anchored in the Mississippi close to St. Bernard Parish, appears so large that you can see it looks like a skyscraper on its side taking up the horizon. It looks closer than it is because the waterline is high. We get closer, and the battleship continues to dominate the skyline.

The air is sweltering and horrible. With New Orleans comes a smell like I've never experienced before. It's thick and putrid. It smells of rotten fish, human feces, fuel, and another odor that I can't pinpoint.

The highway is flooded. We're driving on elevated grass and through some dark patches of water.

Abandoned, partially sunken cars around us give an idea of how deep the water is. In some cases, the water reaches the windows of my Hummer. How this engine isn't flooded baffles and amazes me.

As we move forward, what I'm smelling finally occurs to me. The fourth odor is human flesh rotting in the September sun.

Besides the smell of cooking guts, feces, and fuel, it's a beautiful day.

The smell is working on all of our nerves, though. The battleship on the horizon keeps getting bigger, like a floating city. We pass a vast bridge that leads to nowhere. It simply disappears into the water.

We stop and talk to several U.S. Army Corps engineers that were assessing bridge damage. On the bridge, several sailboats were 40 feet above the water line.

After talking and taking pictures with the U.S. Army Corps engineers, multiple police cars are speeding towards us with dust flying. They are moving with a sense of urgency. We stop.

They're state troopers from Georgia.

All of the state troopers step out. One trooper barks, "Hey! Who's in charge?"

"That'd be me, sir." I respond.

"I have a question!" The trooper responds. "Can we go on the bridge?"

I look at my team members. They look at me.

Feeling nervous, I respond, in my best commanding Bryant Gumbel voice, "Uh, yeah, the bridge is fine. The bridge is fine. There are some engineers.

"Thanks!" They all turn to leave. We head to our van and Hummer.

The State Trooper yells, "Hey!"

At this moment, I thought we may be questioned for being unauthorized civilians in a Martial Law region. I turn around with trepidation and faced the trooper.

He says, "Can we take a picture with you guys?"

With a sigh of relief, I answer, "Yes sir."

All team members, at this point, take a deep breath realizing the law enforcement officers are interested in taking pictures with us and not checking or challenging our credentials. We take a picture and chat a bit afterwards. They ask us where we are going.

"We're going downtown."

"Really?"

"Yeah," I respond.

"We're not goin' that way.

We head out.

The battleship looms greater than ever. We pull our vehicles near the landing zone where a police helicopter just landed. We park and step out. We intended to ask for directions.

The first guy who exits the helicopter appears to be Boss Hogg from the Dukes of Hazard, wearing a cowboy hat and a sheriff's badge.

He looks right at me and yells. "Hey! Who are you with! We're the St. Bernard Parish Sheriff's department!"

"We're Detroit Threat Management!"

"Can you form a perimeter and protect us until the Sheriff's convoy is able to find us?"

"Yes, we can!"

I turn towards my team and stick with the same official-sounding tone. "Form a perimeter!"

"What's a perimeter?"

I lower my voice a bit. "Go over there and form a semi-circle around the helicopter."

Boss Hogg approaches, and we chat.

He says, "We've been cut off from the world. We are bringing satellite phones from the capital. We appreciate the help."

Approximately fifteen minutes pass, and we notice a convoy of several S.U.V.s approaching. This was the Sheriff of St. Bernard Parish and his heavily armed escort. The Sheriff approaches very professionally, introduces himself, and thanks me for providing protective services for the Sheriff's helicopter until he was able to arrive.

He hands me signed documentation. It's legal authorization for our presence in New Orleans. He explains that no one is allowed to be in St. Bernard Parish without the Sheriff's department's permission. That means feds, police, F.E.M.A., anyone. Anyone not allowed to be there is subject to possible arrest on-site.

The Sheriff gives us directions further downtown. We pull out of the landing zone and immediately notice another helicopter traveling in the same direction we were advised to travel by the Sheriff.

On the Mississippi, there's a huge warehouse and a huge manmade boat dock with an industrial-sized boat ramp. Inside there are two to three hundred officers in black tactical uniforms. The words 'Camp Katrina' is painted on a four by six-foot board hanging in the air. This is where the St. Bernard Parish Sheriff instructed us to join with current law enforcement operations.

My team and I park the Hummer and the van. National Guard comes over to greet us. We're talking when another helicopter comes down. It's a smaller, news-caster looking helicopter.

I'm curious, so I head over towards it. Officers are very politely stepping out of my way. As I keep going, I notice they are looking at me. I feel a bit like Moses or maybe General Patton. The helicopter's rotor blade stops, the door opens, and John Travolta steps out with his wife.

I tell Mr Travolta I'm from Detroit.

He's friendly. "Thank you for what you're doing, helping these people, that's great me and my wife are here to show support towards law enforcement officers."

I take a few pictures with John Travolta and his wife. Everyone is looking at me. They think I'm John Travolta's protective detail. To my credit, I walk with a matter-of-factness. I may not know what I'm doing, but I believe in what I'm doing and am willing to die to save families.

A few minutes later, a team member gets my attention. "Hey, uh, there's a guy here with the SEAL team that wants to talk to you."

"SEAL team?"

"Yeah."

"Right. OK. SEAL Team."

A guy walks up to me. "I'm with the SEAL team." He says he's chief master, whatever. I don't believe a word of it.

He keeps talking and repeating himself. "I'm with the SEAL team. We're going to be inserted over here…."

Is this guy coast guard or what?

"I would like you to assist with the SEAL team to assist with the Zodiacs coming over the levee." He continues.

"Sure, I'll help the SEAL team. Of course." I give up.

I think this is some fake sh*t. This is some country-bumpkin coast guard. I don't know where these country guys are coming from. I'm a city guy. I'm not a country guy. I don't know what he's trying to pull, but it's pretty stupid.

Mr Fake SEAL Team walks off. I dutifully turn to my team and mock him.

I'm distracted when I see Hans, one of my guys, walking around with his shoes off. People are looking at him. I hurry over.

"Hans, listen to me, man. We're in a place where there are serious bacteria floating. There's serious agents here. You have to put your shoes on because it's unsafe."

"OK? And please STOP picking your toes."

"Oh, OK."

We're approached a few minutes later. A member of the Coast Guard is with the barge that's anchored alongside the warehouse. He wants to help us launch our boats.

"We could use this crane to get your boats in the water."

My team and I climb up and onto the barge. About thirty men are working, loading, and offloading. I'm soon told to meet the captain.

I crawl through the center rear of the barge and climb up a ladder 30 feet into the air. Up top, there's a semi-military-looking pilothouse. I make my way up and briefly meet captain so-and-so. He's in the middle of something and turns towards a map on the wall.

"OK, here are the kill zones."

Wain what?

"This is the kill zone for the sheriff's department." He indicates a place on the map. "This is the kill zone for the police department." He points again.

"This is a kill zone for—"

My brain is reeling.

This is crazy! There are kill zones here!

I'm mustering my most official appearance and demeanor, but the captain must have noticed something.

"Don't worry, we have a copy for you." He hands me a copy of the kill zones. "We'll help you launch your boats."

The men on board the ship stop what they are doing. The crane swings into motion and our boats are attached, lifted, and placed in the water.

Once the boats are afloat, I realize I don't have much of a team with me.

I'm not sure how this is supposed to play out.

We climb off the barge, and a member of the National Guard approaches us.

"Hey, I just want to let you know. They're planning on taking your truck as soon as you go out into the water."

What?

I attempt to process the situation.

John Travolta's helicopter is over there. I just heard about kill zones.

Now, I'm hearing that some local police are planning to tow away and commandeer my vehicle under Martial Law.

The boats are loaded into the water. I have some decisions to make. 100 Jag has his AR-15 out. He's good to go, ride or die. I'm carrying my 12-gauge SPAS 12 tactical shotgun. I look towards Greg, the boxer. I tell him he must stay with the dog and the vehicles to ensure our stuff is safe.

"I knew it! I knew you planned to deuce me!" Greg yells.

I'm confused. "What are you talking about?"

"I'm not going to be able to go! F*ck this, man! F*ck this!"

He's freaking out, and I can hardly believe it.

This is just what I need.

"It's bullsh*t, man! I need to be going, too!" He continues.

"You will be!"

"Man, f*ck that! F*ck that!"

"You gotta standby, man. I can't take you in the boats right now. We have to make sure we can leave here. After that, we're going to go on a mission, OK?"

"This is bullsh*t, man. I gotta stay with the f*ckin' dog? Bullsh*t, man."

He's understandably upset, but I don't know what he expects me to do. If we don't have vehicles, we don't have a way to get home. Every last dollar I own is in my pocket. I have nothing else to my name. I can't lose my vehicle.

Greg stays with the vehicles. The rest of us climb up the barge, across, and down to the boats.

Before we get in, Brian starts freaking out.

"What are we doing? What's going on?"

"We're going to go rescue people. We're going to get in the boats and go rescue people."

"But how can we do that? If the water is contaminated, the bacteria is 50,000—a million times, ya know, more, bacteria, you heard you can die having contact with this water!"

"I understand that Brian. You knew that when you came down here. We're going to help people."

"But we can get sick, we can die! I can't do it, I can't do it!"

He wants to get out of the boat, which leaves one person in one boat and two in the other.

I think about it. I can't do that. This isn't going to work.

I ask the guys on the ship if they could use the crane to bring the boats back.

"No, we can't do that. What you can do is take your stuff down to the end of the docks and use the boat launch."

It's an industrial boat launch about two football fields wide and just as long. We've got small boats with small engines.

F*ck it; we'll just drive out.

It takes a while, but we drive the boats down to the ramp along with the trucks and trailers. Once we get the boats loaded out of the water and on the trailers, a team member says, "Hey, the Navy guy's back."

"What?"

"Yeah, he's got a bunch of guys with him."

There are about 20 people with the 'SEAL Team guy.

Holy sh*t, this is real.

"I'm with the U.S.S. Tortuga. Our team will be inserted tomorrow morning . We need your assistance getting boats over the levee."

This guy is a Master Chief working with the barge captain to facilitate everything at Camp Katrina. He and his 20 staff members do represent the SEAL Team.

I gather my team. 100 Jag gets in the back of the truck. "Commander, the SWAT team commander wants to talk with you. He wants to know if you're supposed to be armed."

Thirty cops have surrounded the Hummer. They're eyeing the vehicle, chatting with each other. "Man, this is sweet!"

An older officer comes forward. "You guys are, uh, Detroit Threat Management, right?"

"Yes, sir."

"And you guys are all supposed to be armed?"

"Absolutely."

The officer turns around. "They're supposed to be armed!" He turns back towards me. "Where you guys going?"

"SEAL Team base."

"SEAL Team base?"

"Yeah."

The kill-zone map was meant to provide directions. That is the extraction point for the Zodiacs, inflatable black military boats. It shows us where we are expected to bring the vehicles on the actual physical level.

On the way to the levee, I notice a semi-truck with the words ' B.T. Towing'.

Man, we have that in Detroit. Same colors. Interesting. Small world. I guess they have B.T. Towing down here, too.

Next, I see a massive food truck. On the side reads, 'Steve's Soul Food.'
What! That's from Detroit!

"V.I.P.E.R.S.! What are y'all doin' down here?"

It's Steve, who owns the food truck and a few restaurants and night-clubs in Detroit. He's been a client of ours. Within minutes, my team and I are inhaling the best chicken and rice I've ever had. I'm blown away.

***

The Katrina mission brought plenty of unexpected obstacles. A few members of my team proceeded to freak out because we hadn't worked together before. A minor mutiny was not one that I expected.

V.I.P.E.R.S. and I have a rapport based on training, education, and experience. Two of the men on the mission have never received any training from me. When you train someone effectively, you establish a belief in your competence within the trainee. They know you are a sound and capable leader. The two men who weren't V.I.P.E.R.S. didn't know if I was indeed competent. It wasn't precisely the water or other danger that made them go against me. The threat was merely what triggered their doubt.

Chapter 29 Lessons

- The more professional you look, talk and walk, the more professional people will perceive and treat you.
- The Hummer H2 is an excellent automobile that exceeded engineering expectations.
- To effectively lead people, they must have first-hand knowledge of your competence.

30
Motors and Men: The NOLA - Katrina Mission

Part 2

New Orleans, Louisiana

September 2005

We have strict orders to arrive at the secret SEAL team base on the levee. The map says to follow the levee, which means having to drive on top of it. It's little more than a concrete slab jutting up from the ground. It runs for miles over land and across bodies of water. It's approximately six feet wide the entire way.

Occasionally, the levee does disappear.

At one point, we see a group of men in the street. They are all armed. The words "S.B.P.S.D.", which stands for Saint Bernard Parish Sheriff's Department" appear hand-written with black magic marker on dirty white t-shirts they're wearing. These are deputized friends and family members of the Sheriff's department.

We drive slowly. I wave. They don't make eye contact. I sense some kind of inappropriate activity is going on with these guys.

They are walking between what looks to be an oil refinery machinery located on the banks of the river and a modern structure that looks like an office building damaged by the storm. We also saw females that looked distraught walking in proximity of the men. The females had blonde hair and were approx. 20-25 years of age. They appeared to be happy. I was unsure if it was related to the storm or the men they were around.

Nearby, I spot porta-potties. Feces are piled around the structures. We keep driving.

Twenty or thirty men and boys are heavily armed here and there. Filth and fallen houses are everywhere.

We hand out supplies, food, and water to whoever we can along the way.

We pass by a building, and something catches my eye: fish, three stories up, are trapped between the screens and the windows.

We continue until we get to where the levee ramps down to ground level.

I've got to drive my H2 onto and down the levee the rest of the way. The ramp is very steep. Fortunately, we left the van behind, so we only need to get one vehicle onto the structure.

I'm in the Hummer and wondering how I can do this without flipping the vehicle and the boat.

I order everyone to get out. I drive forward as slowly and steadily as possible. The front wheels are barely on the ledge, but I make it up.

My team members climb back in, and we roll on, careful not to buck left or right. It's almost the same width as my vehicle.

The sun goes down, and there are no streetlamps or electricity to be seen in any direction, only my headlights. Ahead, I see something obstructing our path on the levee. I think it's a pile of debris.

A voice yells, "Stop!"

I stop the Hummer, kill the lights, and switch to night vision. Armed men are moving around the trash heap and toward us. My team member is standing in the back of the Hummer, which has a truck bed leaned forward on the roof of the truck with his weapon in a ready position, saying, "There are men in the barricade."

The voices boom back. "Don't lift your weapon" Who are you guys with?"

"We're Detroit Threat Management."

They can see our name and logo on the side of the Hummer.

"We're National Guard. What are you guys doing here?"

"We're on the way to a SEAL team rally point."

"We gotta talk to my N.C.O. before we can let you through. One of you can dismount, approach, and talk to the N.C.O."

I get out and walk up. Ahead there's a fort-like structure standing against the levee. Inside, there's a group in full battle fatigues. They're on high alert as they escort me to the commanding officer.

"Sorry about that out there. We didn't mean to startle you. We had a situation with some guys dressed like us. Once about twenty or thirty got in, we realized they aren't National Guard. They pull out guns and start shooting. We had a shootout. They were a gang trying to infiltrate us."

I realize what the debris barricade was for. They have it spaced on either side of the fort to act as a lock system. The gang must have been after their armory.

After our chat, they move the barricades for the Hummer to get through.

We drive on until we finally make it into what must be a warehouse district. I don't see any people or movement. Everything looks weird. Scenes from zombie movies flash in my mind. I consult the map, but it doesn't show distances.

We roll on cautiously.

A drawbridge can be seen ahead that connects to some kind of marina. Blinding lights hit us.

"Do not move!" a voice yells in very hostile broken English. "Don't you move! You put hands where can see!"

I can make out men in shooting positions. I think I see U.S. Army uniforms.

"What you doing here? Don't move. You have weapons. Where are weapons? Don't reach for weapons. Keep hands up. Don't move hands for any reason."

I'm having a hard time making out the commands. The voice's spoken English grammar isn't excellent, but his accent is very heavy.

"You will listen to my voice. We will verify why you here."

A few minutes go by. My team and I are beyond tense.

These guys almost sound eager to shoot us.

"OK, you can come in. We had to make sure. I'm sure you understand. We had to verify."

Everyone relaxes, and we make our way into the structure.

The men in fatigues are from a Puerto Rican U.S. military police unit. They are assigned to this marina. In Puerto Rico, they're all police officers.

They're nice guys; the atmosphere is festive. We chat and hang out. They offer us cots. Some of us stay up and talk tactics before lying down.

Morning comes around. We receive information that the SEAL team wants us at the locks. We load up and head out.

When we arrive at the locks, I see the operations building that handles it behind a chain-link fence. I give orders to a teammate to check it out. He exits the vehicle and scales a fence.

A man steps out of the building, pointing a 9mm at my teammate.

"Don't move! Who are you?"

"We're with the SEAL team."

I'm not very happy. This guy doesn't understand that if I had perceived him as an actual threat, we would have immediately opened
fire from the Hummer on him. We could have shot through his
entire building.

I can see the guy is stressed, though, and speak up. "We're trying to
get the levee open for the SEAL team. They are coming here right
now."

He lowers the gun and seems a bit more collected. "Well, we can
open it."

"You can?"

"We have our own internal combustion engine. It's off the power
grid. We don't use the power from the city."

"OK."

The SEAL team and the Zodiacs are floating on the other side of
the levee. There are five or six boats, each packed with men in uniforms. They look ready to shoot. There's no room for anyone else
in the boats.

This doesn't look like a rescue operation at all.

I'm asked to spread my team out into different zodiac boats. Then,
a 6'6" John Wayne look-alike approaches. He's a Commander and a
full bird Colonel of an 82nd airborne unit. We exchange greetings

and talk to make sense of the situation.

"We're airborne. I don't know why they want us here. We're not rescuers. My boys are killers. We just got back from Iraq. We were shooting people. I'm not sending my guys in to attack American people."

The Commander requires all rifles to be unloaded, and no ammunition will be issued.

They all have sidearms, Beretta 92 S.P.

My team and I load into the boats. The locks open, and we cross into the city, heading towards the 9th Ward, which was flooded.

The waterline is just above the average car. In each boat, there's someone in the bow using a paddle. They're holding it tilted down, into the water, at approximately a 45-degree angle to gauge the depth. Every once in a while, we see a car, and we can't let the Zodiacs' motors tear into a car's roof. For this reason, we're moving slowly. Whenever the front sailor yells hood or a dead body, the motor is disconnected; the boat driver then holds the back of the engine and tilts it up until we pass through.

The water is everywhere. It's in the streets, between houses, and in every direction. All around me is an apocalypse, and I'm floating quietly through it.

We start to find bodies in the water. Every one of them is bloated and white just below the surface. They tether the bodies to something nearby and leave a piece of neon tape on the road sign or post sticking out of the water.

The air is hot, thick with stench, and silent. Occasionally, we hear the distant baying of a dog. We assume the dogs are trapped but don't know where. A few dogs are spotted on top of cars. Some soldiers encourage them, and the dogs paddle up to the boats.

Our boat comes to a fence that runs along a building. We want to check inside, so we walk the top of the fences, like circus tightrope walkers and make a leap to front porches, or some other entry point. We look around but don't find signs of life in most places.

For miles, there's water and no land. Suburban streets, gas stations, houses, and water just above the cars. We come to a bridge with a truck on it, but we don't see any people.

The bridge opening is wide enough to accommodate our flotilla of 8 boats. The bottom of the bridge disappears on both sides into the water of unknown depth. A few men, including myself, walk up to look for anyone who may be trapped on top.

Two African-American men appear a few yards away. One is big, between 300 and 350 pounds. The other is a bit smaller. They look intense and not like they want to be rescued.

One of the paratroopers' approaches. The two men are eyeing his gun.

I don't like how they're standing. Their postures say nothing about basic respect.

To become a paratrooper, you must weigh less than 220 pounds, or you will not be allowed to enter the Airborne school and jump. The two men eyeing the airborne soldier are much larger.

I walk up and greet them. My tone is strong and authoritative but friendly. Immediately, I feel a change in their energy. They're no longer sizing up the paratroopers.

They lose interest.

"We don't need any help; we don't need nothin'."

"We've got a place to stay, beds, hot showers, everything you need aboard the U.S.S. Tortuga, and we can have a boat take you there now." I respond.

"Nah, we're good." They turn and leave.

I believed that these individuals, who did not have a shower or clean food and water for five days, were Marauders. They were praying for men, women, and children, so they did not want to leave the area.

We walk up the bridge at its highest point, which is 50 feet above the water. Further inspecting the area around the truck, I see signs of habitation. A small group of people are assembled here. People could be trapped inside the trucks or, even worse, held against their will. I started to look around intensely because it made no sense that these seven men were sitting on a bridge in weather that was over 100 degrees, not looking for shelter for safety.

An older man steps out of the truck. I must have caught his attention when I spoke to the two men.

"I saw a barge that exploded and that breached the levee."

This man is between 75 and 80 years old.

"I've seen them do it four other times. They let the water flood the port. But I've never seen anything like this, not this bad. I saw the barge come in. I saw them blow the levee with my own eyes."

The youngest male on the bridge began to tell a story about people being attacked at a school. H stated they were hurting the children. Kids were on the top floor, and these guys just came there and assaulted them."

"How do you know that?" I asked.

He balks like he doesn't understand the question.

"There's no phones. So, how did you know?"

He doesn't respond.

Something is wrong with this story.

The young man speaks up. "Yeah, yeah. We gotta get those kids out of there."

"Show us where to go." I said.

We transport the young guy with us into the boats and head towards the school.

Along the way, one of the Navy guys decides to brave the water. He'll give the boats a safe path to follow if he can slosh through the debris. We can get to school faster. He avoids having to swim and stays as shallow as possible. Mostly, his boots are the only part of him submerged.

This water is putrid beyond imagination but shallow, yet we can still get trapped.

When our boats pull up to a point where we can go on foot, I'm asked to pull the boat's motor up. That means I have to put my hand in the water akin to bacterial lava. One of the sailors just told me a story of another sailor that was flown to a hospital from a ship because he had a cut on his foot that became infected when it was exposed to the water, causing his foot to expand to twice its normal size within minutes of contacting the water.

"I can't do that." I spoke.

They keep asking, and I keep saying, "I can't do that."

Eventually, I give in. I reach in. The water is horrible. I pull up the engine.

We arrive at Thomas Edison Elementary School. Approximately 10 of us scale the building to the top window. It's empty, with no kids. However, it appears people were staying up here. The place is disheveled and nasty.

We talk to the young guy in the tractor-trailer, but he's not giving any further information. We don't press him too much, and he provides us with another story.

I get a call on my radio from a team member. He's asking permission to shoot a lock somewhere in Ninth Ward.

I respond, "Absolutely not. Do not discharge your weapon." I reason that he's not legally authorized to shoot anyone unless an exigent circumstance exists.

One of the Navy guys with my teammate uses his M14 to blast the lock.

We hear the gunshot.

The rest of the day, we motor around in the zodiac. It's uneventful. The sun starts going down, and we head back.

We then join at a rallying point with the other flotilla of 8 zodiac boats with approximately six men on each boat. Sixteen zodiacs and 96 men, 40 % U.S. Navy, 40% U.S. Airborne, 15% Sheriff's and 5% V.I.P.E.R.S.

We make it back to the boat ramp without incident. I overhear one of the military units confirming one gunshot.

"That was not a gunshot. That was a lock-shot." I interrupt and explain it was one of the Navy guys.

Is the Navy not communicating with the other departments?

Our team stays overnight at the base. The next day, we load into my Hummer H-2 SUT and head towards the Superdome. On the way, we see Armored Personnel Carriers with men gathered on top of the vehicles. Altogether we see about twenty A.P.C.s. These are Vietnam-era military vehicles. There's a noticeable lack of diversity among the men mounting these vehicles. I'm trying to make sense of it.

I see guys pointing M4s while driving through neighborhoods yelling, "Mandatory evacuation, come out! Come out of your homes! Come out now!"

These men are in shooting positions. I can't imagine anyone wanting to come out of their home to something like that. Anyone inside those homes would be terrified.

On our way out of New Orleans, we see various people and organizations along the road. We occasionally stop to see if anyone needs assistance or supplies. We gave supplies to families; this included rubbing alcohol, water, and M.R.E. (meals ready to eat) military. There were kids, senior citizens and families with small children, all from different ethnic groups. We spot John Walsh walking in boots from America's Most Wanted with Sheriff's deputies. He's very positive and professional in person.

Downtown, we see some police officers who are ending their shifts. We greet them. They look exhausted. A car pulls up, and a guy steps out.

"Hey, can you take me through New Orleans?"

I apologize. Unfortunately, we don't have any room.

He explains he's with the L.A. Times. "C'mon, just take me with you, and I'll get you guys' international notoriety."

"I wish I could, but I really can't take anyone."

He showed his credentials, and I thought about it but refused because I did not want to take responsibility for another life in an exceedingly dangerous surrounding; we also don't have the room.

Finding our way out of downtown New Orleans takes a little while. We drive slow. I'm becoming more aware of how stressed my body and brain are. It's completely unsafe here. No electricity, communication, working hospitals, firefighters, or police service exists. Society is not functioning down here.

We're low on gas. I hit the OnStar button and get someone on the line.

"Where's the nearest gas station?"

We get directions, arrive at the pump, and there's no gas.

I press the OnStar button again and get directions to another station. "Can you verify that they have gas?"

"Yes, but I also verified the last one."

OnStar's info is out of date. We're very low on gas and driving around Nowhere, Louisiana.

An hour and a half away from the highway, we find a gas station that has fuel. Now, it's time to eat.

We drive back out of the boonies and hit a diner near the highway. The place is full of cops. We sit at a table, and I notice we're getting some stares. I look to my team, and I see Hans is barefoot again.

"Hans, where are your shoes?"

"Oh, I took them off 'cuz my feet were uncomfortable."

"What are you doing in a restaurant with your shoes off?"

This is bullsh*t.

"Go get your shoes on, please. You can't seriously be in a restaurant with your shoes off." I continue.

A couple of firefighters pull up and settle in. In a thick southern accent, one of them says, "Hey, you guys are welcome to go to our fire station and shower and rest up." We give nods and say 'hi.'

I'm a bit paranoid. We're still in what looks like Deliverance, Louisiana.

Gamma-14 is more paranoid. "Man, I'm not going there, getting lynched. We gotta get outta here."

In my mind, I agree. *No, no. Nope. I am not getting lynched.*

The firefighter protests, "Man, it ain't like that no more. You guys are fine, fine."

He's smiling a lot.
We've got to get the f*ck out of here.

And we do. The rest of the trip happens without incident. We will be back in Michigan within 24 hours. This was the end of our mission. We accomplished bringing needed supplies to families of all ethics groups. A total of 40 hours in New Orleans and 50 hours of driving to and from New Orleans.

****

Much of Detroit can be dangerous. As you've read, I've experienced plenty of life-threatening situations there. The danger in New Orleans in September of 2005 was on another level. It wasn't a crime-ridden city. It was a manmade dystopian apocalypse by design. I will never forget it; the pungent odors, the heavy silence and the distinct absence of birds singing, the stunningly beautiful sunshine, the hot and muggy air, and the best-tasting chicken and rice I've ever had.

Our mission opened my eyes to a new reality. Humans do not do well without law enforcement. Government and law enforcement must be accessible. Without these things, society crumbles and turns on itself rapidly.

The private sector must be used for private matters such as corporate situations. The public must take responsibility for their safety by having community-prepared rescue teams.

You must have a government, but you cannot be solely dependent on the government. You must be willing and capable of providing the protection needed during natural disasters.

The public must rescue itself, and there must be active law enforcement providers. Each is essential, and each must be separate. It can be harmful and counterproductive to attempt to focus on both enforcing laws and rescue operations.

The different military and state factions were not in communication with each other. Nobody knew who was in charge.

A strong sense of purpose is required in high-stress, chaotic situations with multiple factions at work. If I had to pick a favorite, the Navy guys were a lot of fun. I was in a boat full of comedians. The energy was very positive.

What people want is protection. What we need are protectors.

Chapter 30 Lessons

- Protectors care about people.
- Society is held together by commonly held beliefs that are quickly for-gotten under life-threatening conditions from natural disasters.
- Without electricity and communication, many people will lose a sense of reality, resulting in various acts of inhumanity.

31
Seven-Mile Dogs

Detroit Michigan

The River Rock Club

A gang attacks people one night at the River Rock Club. VIPERS, who are paid security for the club, kick them out.

The gang yells threats. They outnumber us two to one—a VIPER wall forms.

"Target."

Each VIPER points to a specific gang member.

"Engage."

*

Gangs in Detroit often name themselves after streets. The gang calls themselves the Seven-Mile Dogs. They're not a familial gang; there's no leadership hierarchy. There's no head to remove. Each member is a micro-cell with no idea who to trust within the organization. They hardly trust the people they know, making them easy to infiltrate.

Detroit is dangerous because of gangs like this, but, these gangs form because there is no respect for anything. Criminals don't respect other criminals.

Police officers began supporting the VIPERS in 1998 and 99 because we had their backs when they went to nightclubs. The VIPERS protect police officers from assault and harassment. If someone threatens a cop, we throw them out. If a dispute arises between a cop and another patron, we take the cop's word and side with them.

*

The VIPERS charge, like in the movie Braveheart, into the crowd of Seven-Mile Dogs. During the scuffle, one gang member runs straight into a police lieutenant's car and clips the mirror.

I'm not at the fight. I'm somewhere else. I get a call and show up.

The fighting has subsided, and the L.T. is standing by his vehicle. He's irate.

The L.T. cusses me out. "Look at my mirror!"

I see the mirror's broken. "Oh! I can get you some super glue. I can glue it back on there for you."

"What? No! Your men just did that!"

"OK, I'm sorry. I'm sure if they did that, there's a good reason—"

"No! There's no good reason to chase people and attack them and have them knock a mirror off my car."

"OK, sir, may I check it out."

"You can check all you want! If you ever fight outside again, you're going to get arrested. You are not to fight outside the nightclubs. You are not to put your hands on people no matter what happens. If you fight under any conditions outside the nightclub, you are to be arrested."

"Sir, can I just talk to my guys really quick?"

I check in with VIPERS and ask them what happened.

"Yes, sir, we were standing there on our wall. They attacked us. We attacked back. One of them ran away from us and hit the car. We never touched the guy. He just ran and hit the car, trying to get away from us."

Ten gang squad officers are standing out front with the VIPERS. I walk back to the L.T. He's facing me while his officers stand behind him. They are making hand signals that imply no hard feelings or to let things go.

I proceed to attempt to reason with the L.T. again. "I apologize, sir, but I don't know if you knew this, but the guys attacked my guys, and then my guys followed their structured protocol and attacked them back.

That's when one of the attackers ran, but they attacked our team members first. They swung first."

"What? That's bullsh*t. I was standing right here!"

I check in with VIPERS again. They explain that the L.T. had his back to the VIPERS. He didn't see what was happening.

"Sir, you were looking the other way."

"No—my—look—hey, did any of y'all see it? Did *any* of y'all see one of them attack the VIPERS? Did the VIPERS get attacked? Anybody? Anybody!"
The gang squad members don't respond at first—their heads down. A few mumble, "no, sir."

"See, I told you! Yo men lyin'!"

*Oh, sh*t.*

"That's some bullsh*t!" The L.T. takes off in a black unmarked Crown Victoria with the mirror hanging off it.

I casually approached and spoke with several gang squad members off the record. They seemed to be relieved the L.T. is gone.

"Aw man, your guys did their job, man. They were perfect! They were standing there. Guys were talkn' sh*t, threatening your guys. Your guys didn't say nothing. When they started swinging, that's when your men attacked. You guys were totally disciplined."

"Why didn't you tell him! Why didn't you tell the lieutenant?"

"Man, you can't tell him sh*t! If any of us would have said—if any of us would have said a f*ckin' word, we'd got written up."

*

A week later, the scene in front of the River Rock Club looks like something out of the movie Blackhawk Down. Gang members are chasing people and beating them down. Beatdowns are happening in front of us.

VIPERS just stand there, not fighting and not getting arrested. *I can't do anything.*

I have a new guy with VIPERS. I'm paying him 50 dollars an hour, cash. That's a lot of money in 1997. This guy looks like Kurt Russell as Snake Plissken, but bigger, with two large handguns holstered on his torso. He's a sheriff in a rural community, but he makes more money working with us. He has one job: to stand outside the night-club and shoot the shooters if there is a shooting. Keep us alive.

People are being beaten, stripped, and robbed. Naked bodies are on the ground. We are told not to fight outside of the club.

A sergeant from the gang squad and another lieutenant are sitting in the car by themselves outside the club. They are sitting in their cars, making sure the VIPERS aren't fighting. Respectively they are about 50 and 60 years of age.

A young man, about twenty years old, approaches. "I'll kill all you motherf*ckas. I'll knock you out. I'll f*ck all you up, security."

The VIPERS say nothing besides, "young man, have a nice day."

The guy raises his hand to fight.

"Keep moving, sir. Don't touch us. Everything will be fine. Just don't touch us."

Four random guys mill around outside the club. The angry guy decides to target them. He moves in and starts swinging. He's fast, and a skilled boxer, and he hits all four of them for no reason in particular.

One victim goes down against the lieutenant's car.

The lieutenant, code name Deacon, gets out and puts the victim in a chokehold.

The thug says, "F*ck all you motherf*ckas. F*ck the police. F*ck you mother*ckas." He directs his attention to the VIPERS. "I'll f*ck y'all ass up. Step to me, any of y'all. I do you like I just did him."

VIPERS want to attack, but they don't.

The Deacon is choking the victim out.

Detroit Police Sergeant, codename Broderick, steps out.
The boxer thug rushes him and punches him to the ground. The L.T. lets go of the victim and move into the assailant.

The angry young guy backs off and walks away.

One of the four victims approaches the VIPERS. "Why didn't you guys help us!"

"The police won't let us help you. I apologize. I wish I could have helped you, but you can make a complaint to the police."

"I'm going to complain."

"I wouldn't complain here. I would go to the police station. Not necessarily here."

I approach Deacon. "Hey, uh, ya know that guy you were choking was a victim?"

"What?"

"Yeah, he got hit. He was knocked halfway unconscious. He had already been struck in the skull, and he was falling. The reason he hit your car is he was punched—yeah, the guy just got hit, was trying to grab onto the car, before you got out—"

A young African-American man walks up wearing a cream Izod sweater with a Polo button-down shirt, khaki pants, and penny loafers with pennies and no socks. He's very articulate when and reminds me of a kid in law school or a lawyer's son.

"Excuse me, sir. I respectfully ask for your name and badge number."

I was thinking; No, don't. Please, just go away.

"What'd you say?" said the Lt.

"Sir, I respectfully ask for your name and badge number."

I explain what's going on with the L.T. "That's the friend of the guy you were choking."

The L.T. grabs the conservative kid by the throat, lifts him, and choke-slams him at my feet. "Now, what do you want?"

"I wanna go, I just wanna go."

"That's what I thought. Go on, now."

Wow, I just saw this lieutenant choke a victim. Then choke-slam a kid who respectfully asked for a name and badge number.

*

One day later, I witnessed the same Sargent advise stop an Afri-can-American guy in a truck.

"You gotta move your truck."

The guy appears to ignore him.

"Hey, not gonna tell you again, gotta move your truck."

"Man, you can say what the f*ck you want. I ain't movin' sh*t."

"Aight, you gonna get a ticket."

"Give me the mother f*ckin' ticket, mother*cker. You know what, you got a smart mouth, motherf*cker, gimme my motherf*ckin' ticket and shut the f*ck up."

"Get back in the car."

"Put me back in the car"

"You got a real attitude problem."

"Do somethin' about it, gimme my ticket, shut the f*ck up, Gimme my sh*t and don't f*ckin' talk to me. I got money. I'll pay this sh*t. Now you shut the f*ck up, you a public servant. Gimme my f*ckin' ticket, get the f*ck out my face. That's the f*ck you can do." Truck-guy looks at me. "Whatchoo goin' do?"

"Well, nothin' if you don't do anything."

"Whatever, I'll do the f*ck I want. You better not touch me."

"Sir, I promise you, if you touch that officer or if you touch me, I will definitely touch you. I promise you, upfront, don't touch him. Don't touch me."

"You ain't gotta worry about that. Ima' tell you like this; you touch me, I'll put both ya asses in jail. I'll sue both you mother*ckas. I'll have yo job."

"If you touch him, or you touch me, you're going to be hurt right now. On the ground. You understand?"

"Man, shut the f*ck up talkn' to me.. You got my ticket?

I'm enraged and outraged. The lieutenant, this cop, is not beating the hell out of this guy because why?

Choke-slam him! Get out of the car and choke-slam him!

Deacon is sitting in the squad car writing the ticket. Truck-guy stands outside Deacon's window.

That's completely tactically ignorant, unintelligent, breach of protocol procedure—I can't f*cking believe this. Can you beat someone's ass, please? Officer, do your thing. This is the time to beat someone up. Beat him up, go, I'll even help you!

I speak under my breath to Deacon, "Hey, uh, you wanna put this guy in custody? Ya know, I got your back."

"Nah, nah. We're good. F*ck it."

Deacon hands him the ticket out the window. Truck-guy snatches it out of the lieutenant's hand.

" I still ain't movin'." He gets back in the truck.

You'll choke-slam a kid that didn't do sh*t. But this man who is disorderly, violently threatening you, a police officer, and you won't do sh*t? Really?

I'm furious.

***

The officer with two guns on his hips said he could not work with us for any amount of money because of the violence he saw.

The events affected me psychologically. I witnessed brutality. I think of myself as a good person. I say I like to help and protect people. I didn't protect that kid. I have to live with that. I have to live with the fact that I allowed people to be abused and brutalized in front of me.

You may have gleaned by now that I am an individual in a state of protest. My life is one protesting the abuse of people.

I didn't understand the disparity in Deacon's actions in terms of when to use violence. That led to nearly uncontrollable frustration for me. Once I understood why he acted the way he did, I was able to conduct myself accordingly. I was able to realign myself and effectively carry out my mission.

Chapter 31 Lessons
- Do not say or do things that can be considered offensive to a cop or criminal unless you are in the court of law
- Police often face abuse from vile individuals without cause
- After the sergeant was attacked, we were told that we can fight outside of the club without the fear of being arrested.

32
Commander Brown
Part 1

Detroit, Michigan

The Detroit Police Domestic Violence Advocate refers the VIPERS to a young lady. I'm on the phone with the advocate.

"The Police are not helping this victim. We need you to help. This is really serious."

The woman's ex-husband is a United States Marine and a drug dealer.

He's abusive and recently attacked her with a hammer.

The woman was struck in the arm, neck, and face. I'm looking at the pictures; she's a bloody mess.

She escaped by crawling to the neighbor's house.

The judge orders that he still gets visitation rights with the children because he never attacked the kids.

He's now out on bond, and the home is in his name. The mother can't stay with him, so she gets a P.P.O. and stays with a platonic friend.

The woman and her friend are in their 20s. He lives with his mother and has a gun permit. The guy's mom is on board with what's happening.

"You can allow this young lady to live with us in our home and protect her and her children."

The marine ex-husband has visitation rights, so the mother has to take the kids to him without protection. Through contact, the marine figures out the friend has a handgun. He takes the matter to the judge.

"I don't want my children around a person with a gun." Says the marine.

"That's fair. You can't have the gun around children." Says the judge.

"What do you mean? I have a gun permit. I live with my mother. This woman lives with us now. Why would I not have a gun?" Replies the friend.

"Either you move, or she and the children move."

"How will she have protection? Who's going to protect her and the children? What if he comes back with the hammer to kill her and her children this time?"

The judge goes on. "Well, we'll have to see if that happens, but we're not going to allow him to have a gun around the children."

The friend moves out of his mother's house to accommodate the victim and her children.

The young woman works at a government-paid charity that feeds people; The ex-husband stalks her at work, terrorizes and threatens her and her coworkers.

"I'm going to kill everybody up here. I'm going to kill all you b*tches. I'm shooting everybody."

The charity decides to fire her.

"I am a single mother. I have three children. How are you going to fire me because he's terrorizing and threatening me, and trying to kill me? How will I feed my children if you fire me?"

They fire her, and word gets to me. I review the situation and call the charity's office. I ask to speak to the administrator of the entire organization.

"This is Commander Brown from Detroit Threat Management Center." I'm using my Bryant Gumbel voice.

I continue. "We will need to hear from your organization by 5:00 o'clock today before we take any legal action on behalf of Ms. Johnson in reference to being terminated after being terrorized and threatened by her ex-husband. We hope to bring this to closure without legal intervention."

They call back. "What is the meaning of this?"

"Yes, this is Threat Management Center. We don't want to take legal action until we have a chance to let you remedy the situation another way."

"Well, what do you mean?"

"We don't think it'll be a good legal look. The optics, in our opinions, would be damaging to a charitable organization if it's found out that a single mother was fired because she's being terrorized."

They invite me to a meeting with the executive directors and the head of security, a retired chief of Police. The meeting feels like a big deal. The people on the other side of the table seem nervous.

"So, what's going on here?"

I don't hold back. "The situation is what it is. You are a good organization, and we don't think that you should be seen as an organization that does not support women and children who are domestic violence victims. So, is there any way you could put her in a different division—some other place without terminating her employment? Therefore, she still maintains her job, so she can feed her children. And we don't have to continue to escalate this into a situation that would be—not advantageous to the reputation of this organization."

Whispers, murmurs, and nervous energy go around the room. They finally reply.

"What about having her in a bulletproof tower with tinted windows, so you won't even know she's there?"

"Can she hide her vehicle somewhere?" I asked.

"Yes, there's actually indoor parking in another spot!"

The young woman gets her job back. She works in security in a bulletproof, darkened tower. She's free.

***

This story may be unbelievable to you. How could a charity organization do such a thing to single mothers and employees? How could a judge make a ruling like the one he did? How could the ex-husband, a man trained in violence, get off so easy for beating a woman with a hammer? Many of the stories in this book are difficult to entertain because they run contrary to our perception of reality.

Well, in the end, he didn't get off so easy. A year after the woman regained her position at the charity, the ex-husband went to prison.

I could have confronted the ex-husband, but that would not have helped the mother regain her employment. Instead, I learned to use my voice, my presence, and the phone. I created what I have dubbed an unstoppable win. The young lady and her family won, the charitable organization won before they don't get exposed, and we won because we fulfilled our organization's purpose.

Chapter 32 Lessons

- Legal threats pair well with a Bryant Gumbel voice
- To create an "unstoppable win," you must create three winners.
- Sometimes, it only takes a conversation to keep a family from being destroyed.

33
Commander Brown

Part 2

Detroit, Michigan

A young woman returns home from college to visit her mother. Someone breaks in. The cops get called, and they arrest the man. Then he gets out the next day. There are no charges. He goes back to the apartment building. They live in the same apartment building, on the same floor in adjacent apartments.

After attending her classes at Wayne State University, she goes home, and she is surprised that her neighbor, who broke into her apartment the night before by kicking in the door, is now back in his apartment. He is leaning out of one of the windows, and before she can get to the front door of the apartment building- he opens fire with the pistol.

On the second floor, the woman's mother has an injured foot and can hear the gunshots aimed at her daughter. She calls 911 as her daughter fights for her life by throwing rocks at the gunman.

The rocks she threw caused the gunman to retreat; unfortunately, the rocks damaged the window he was shooting from.

The Police arrive and take him into custody for the second time in two days.

A short time later, the woman gets a call from the apartment building manager they live in.

"You are being put out of government housing for the destruction of property."

"Someone was shooting at me."

"Yeah, but you can't destroy property."

"Someone was *shooting* at me! I had to survive!"

"Ma'am, we don't know anything about that. All that we can tell you is that you threw rocks and damaged the windows and window-panes. That's vandalism. You're being evicted."

I get a call from a women's shelter. They have the young woman who's been put out of her house. The mother has just been released from the hospital. She needs to pick up her mother, but they will have nowhere to go.

I make a call to the manager of the apartment building. No one picks up, so I leave a message.

"This is Commander Brown Detroit Threat Management Center! We have a problem, and before we escalate this legally, we'll give you an opportunity. Information arrived at our desk that you, in fact, plan to evict a girl who was defending herself from a gunman. If this is true that you plan to evict a college student and her injured mother for defending their lives from an armed assailant shooting at them, we need to know this is true before any legal action is taken.

A lawyer calls me back immediately.

"This is counsel for the—" He sounds panicked.

I cut him off and bring my voice from gruff to deep. "This is Threat Management Center. We don't want to take action. We want to work this out. So I would suggest you look at this properly with fresh eyes and get back to us before the end of the day."

"I sure will—"

An hour later, the young woman calls me. "Oh my God, I don't know who you talked to. Oh my God, thank you. Thank you for whatever you did!"

"What are you talking about?" I said.

"We are getting a *house*. We are getting our own house. We were supposed to get an apartment, but they're actually giving us a house because of whatever you did. They're moving us this week to our own *home*. Thank you!"

The woman fills me in on a few more details, and the call ends. I'm shocked.

Wow. That's amazing. These people were evicting them and putting them on the street. Now they are giving them a house in a nice neighborhood.

****

This story echoes some of the previous lessons. Criminals caught red-handed are not correctly charged or processed. They are often released, and they retaliate.

Again, I could have dealt with the gunman directly if I could have found him. Instead, I dealt with the apartment managers. However, my priority was to help the young woman in a dire situation.

Additionally, I was astounded by the bravery of this young woman. When someone starts shooting at you, the first instinct is not to look for rocks to throw. The woman knew her mother was trapped inside.

Chapter 33 Lessons

- Bureaucracy cannot stop you from doing the right thing
- "Let's work this out, so we *don't* have legal problems" is effective when the other party knows it's in the wrong
- Love is the highest form of protection

34
Baby Recovery

Detroit, Michigan

A woman calls. She's crying.

"Please help me; someone broke into our house and took my niece's son."

"Did you call the police." I asked.

"We did. They said there's nothing they can do because the baby's father took him. He went to a hotel. He doesn't even know the baby. The baby is only one month old. He needs breast milk."

The child's mother indicated she is 16, and he is 20. He just got out of prison for armed robbery and burglary.

I head to the police station with the mother to ask the Police to assist her in getting her child back. The Police refuse to send any units unless she can verify where the baby is. I have a documentary crew in tow.

The mother and I get in the Hummer and head for the hotel.

The baby's father is there with multiple drug dealers when we arrive. I call 911.

"They're at the hotel with the baby."

"OK, the 911 operator indicated they will send a unit."

An hour later, the cops pull up. I approach. The police cruiser stops. The cops inside are staring at me. It's an all too familiar scene.

These cops weren't sent here. They just happen to be passing by.

I explain the situation.

"Officers, we know that the baby is here somewhere."

"OK, well, we can't do anything."

"Can you go with us? Just be with us?"

"OK, well. That's fine."

We visit the front desk, head upstairs, and go to the room the men checked into. No one comes to the door. When we turn to leave, we see a woman standing by the elevator. She has the baby.

The mother says. "That's my baby!"

I say. "What are you doing with that baby?"

The Police say, "Yeah, what are you doing with the baby?"

The woman holding the baby says, "Somebody told me to watch the baby."

"Who?" I ask.

"I'unno, I'unno who he was." She responds.

The cops balk. "What?"

The mother marches up and takes the baby from her.

The police press the woman. "What room was he in? What room—"

I interrupt, "gentlemen, gentlemen. We have the baby. So we're going to need to go. We gotta get the *baby* out of here."

The cops respond, "Well, can you wait in the hallway while we go to the room?"

"Sir, we're not going to be able to wait here. We're going to get in the car."

The mother, baby, and I wait in the car. The officers come downstairs a few minutes later.

"OK, good to go?"

"Yep, good to go."

The mother and I leave, but we don't know where to take her. The man is calling her. "I'm coming to the house, and I'm going to kill you and take the baby."

We are calling around to shelters, but the mother is a minor. None of these shelters will accept her.

Finally, we find one shelter that's receptive. It's the only shelter in Michigan that will take her in.

We don't have any money. The young mother doesn't have any money. We drive three hours to the only domestic violence shelter in Michigan that provides shelter for domestic violence minors with children. They assess the situation and take her in. We head back to Detroit.

***

After we helped the young mother, we got in contact with the aunt who originally called us. We asked her how she found out about our organization. She began crying. "I saw you on the news a few years ago. I knew my niece needed help, so I contacted you. I knew your organization would help her. I knew you help her."

At the time, I didn't know that even with the laws broken by the baby's father laws and willing witnesses to prosecute, no one cared to use the laws to protect this young mother and her child.

Chapter 34 Lessons
- The laws in Detroit are often used to prosecute rather than protect.
- Commonly the only reason people receive appropriate assistance is that other people care.

35
Fake Lil' Wayne Terrorist

Detroit, Michigan

A man wants to date a security guard and mother of five. He looks like Lil Wayne, and she's not interested. She looks like the rapper Eve!

He buys a few houses. He offers her one. She doesn't want to date him, so she offers to pay him for the house.

Once she's moved in, he starts demanding a sexual relationship from her. She's not giving in. He goes to visit her.

"You either have to have sex with me, or I'll put you out."

"I'll just leave then." She says.

At the police station, she reports what happened.

"He's my landlord, and I feel threatened, he trying to make me have sex with him instead of paying for rent, and I don't want to do that. I want to pay for my rent. I'm afraid he's going to do something to me."

She goes back to the house. He's breaking in. He comes back that same day.

The woman shoots at him, this time when he gets inside the house. She leaves a bullet hole in the wall next to his head.

"If you take another step forward, I'm going to shoot you. '

The man leaves. She calls the Police to report the break-in.

The Police come to the house, and then he comes to the house. The Police talk to Lil Wayne wannabe lookalike and he tells them she shot at him for no reason. The Police ask her if she has a weapon. She says, "yes, I'm an armed security officer; this is my legally owned gun and I have a permit to carry. He broke into my house, so I shot at him because he endangered me and my children."

The Police then arrest her and take her to jail, and the five children are left with the man inside the house.

While the woman is locked away, the man may have assaulted the children. One of the sergeants finds out what's going on inside the house, but they don't understand the situation. They free the woman but decide to keep her gun.

The woman becomes vocal. "You took me to jail. I'm a victim. I reported this. And now you have my gun and I need to go home and get my children. He is not their father. They do not know him.

The sergeant in charge realizes there is something wrong with the arrest, and decides to release her after two hours- but refused to give her gun back.

The victim goes to her house, and he changed the locks to her home. She bangs on the door- and he opens the door. She notices her 5 kids sitting on the couch, terrified. She rushes in to hold her children, he locks the door, and lunges at her, tackling her to the ground, with her children screaming in horror.

She is raped, in front of her children. After a prolonged period of sexual abuse, he fled the area.

She immediately called the Police.

This time the Police took her side, returned her gun, and helped her get medical treatment. They issued a warrant for his arrest for aggravated rape and home invasion.

The Detroit Police advocate refers her to our organization for sex crimes. After enrolling her in our FREE Victory Protection Program, my wife, 111 Mantis makes a deal with a hotel manager to give a discounted rate to the woman with her five children. We paid for the hotel out of our pocket and secured a $1000 worth of food from a restaurant that is part of our protectorate circle. My team members and I head to the house.

The Hummer pulls up. It's very imposing. It has our logo on it. The guy knows we are there for her and her five children. He's driving an S.U.V., and as I approach the house, he veers toward my vehicle- in a ramming trajectory.

He misses and flees, luckily for him, because my Hummer is a lot heavier and stronger than his Ford S.U.V. We give chase while calling the Police. "He's over here." I provide the plate number and direction of travel as we returned to the house to extract the woman and her five children to a safe location

We transport the mother and her five children to a safe hotel with restricted access.

Approximately four days later, the Police located and arrested him. He goes to prison.

***

What happened to the security guard and mother of five and her children was horrifying.

Chapter 34 Lessons

- It is imperative to avoid conditions that lead to opportunities for violence and predation to occur. We call this Threat opportunity denial.
- The Police should have arrested him because he broke into her house without authorization. They should not have considered this situation domestic violence- because it wasn't.

JENNIFER M. GRANHOLM
GOVERNOR

MARIANNE UDOW
DIRECTOR

02/01/2007

Col. Pete Munoz
Michigan State Police
714 S. Harrison Road
East Lansing, MI. 48823

Dear Col. Munoz,

My name is Joyce Martin, Regulation Manager with the Office of Inspector General (OIG), Department of Human Services (DHS). The Office of Inspector General investigates alleged fraud committed by Welfare Recipients, State Employees and Private Vendors. We have a specialized team of agents who investigates applications prior to benefits being issued. Due to the fact, benefits have not been issued applicants become resentful and defensive when a home call is conducted to verify eligibility factors. On January 29, 2007, Trooper Walter Crider of the Michigan State Police, Dale Brown, Founder of the Threat Management Center & Instructor Lochirco of the Threat Management Center, conducted a Safety Training session for our field agents. Trooper Crider was extremely instrumental in organizing the training session. To prepare for the training Trooper Crider requested a copy of the State of Michigan's Worker Safety Law and a list of potential dangerous situations we have encountered while conducting field investigations.

The Office of Inspector General has attended numerous safety-training classes in the past but the information Trooper Crider organized was more informative, aggressive, reality based and tailored to our specific needs and concerns. The survival tactics demonstrated by Dale Brown and Instructor Lochirco were a true asset. I received positive feedback from the agents during the training and the Kudos continued into the following day.

I plan to recommend that the entire Wayne County Office of Inspector General contact Trooper Crider and request his specialized "Safety Training".

Comments regarding the Training:

Thanks for planning the safety training. It was definitely beneficial and well received by all attendees.

I loved that training! I went home and showed my family all the maneuvers and imitated Dale Brown...he was so---oo funny! I was also much more "aware" at my home call alone...today. Thank Trooper Crider for putting all of that together.

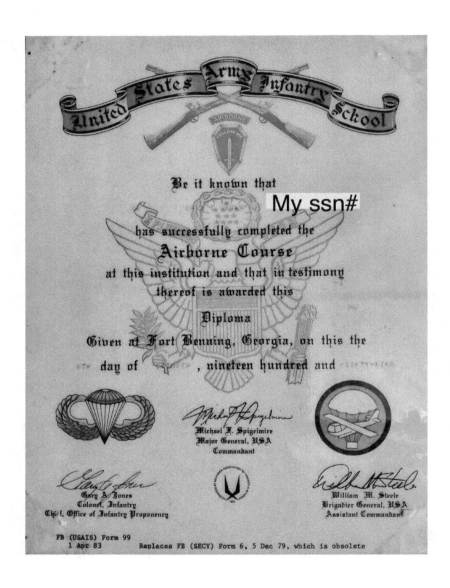

United States Army Infantry School

Be it known that

My ssn#

has successfully completed the

Airborne Course

at this institution and that in testimony
thereof is awarded this

Diploma

Given at Fort Benning, Georgia, on this the

day of , nineteen hundred and

Michael F. Spigelmire
Major General, USA
Commandant

Gary A. Jones
Colonel, Infantry
Chief, Office of Infantry Proponency

William M. Steele
Brigadier General, USA
Assistant Commandant

FB (USAIS) Form 99
1 Apr 83   Replaces FB (SECY) Form 6, 5 Dec 79, which is obsolete

OFFICE OF THE DEAN

UNIVERSITY OF MICHIGAN–DEARBORN
COLLEGE OF ARTS, SCIENCES, AND LETTERS

4901 EVERGREEN ROAD
DEARBORN, MICHIGAN 48128-2406
313 593-5400 FAX 313 593-5552

September 21, 2011

Commander Dale Brown
Threat Management Center
6440 Wight Street
Detroit, MI 48207

Dear Commander Brown:

As the new academic year gets underway I wanted to thank you for your partnership with the Criminal Justice program at the University of Michigan-Dearborn. The program is an exceptionally strong one and its strength is due to the community partnership we have with law enforcement agencies, organizations, and leaders. I appreciate the willingness of our community partners to both refer strong students to the program and to accept interns from the program. I also want to thank you for attending the recognition luncheon held over the summer. As I wound down my first year as Dean it was especially gratifying to meet and see the individuals that help to make our Criminal Justice program a point of pride for the College of Arts, Sciences, and Letters.

Best Regards,

Jerold L. Hale
Dean

DETROIT POLICE DEPARTMENT
TRAINING CENTER PRESENTS THIS

CERTIFICATE OF APPRECIATION

To

DALE C. BROWN

IN APPRECIATION FOR YOUR OUTSTANDING SERVICE AND SUPPORT TO THE CITY OF DETROIT
AND OUR COMMUNITY CELEBRATING THE DETROIT POLICE ACADEMY'S
100TH YEAR ANNIVERSARY.

JULY 8, 2011
DATE

COMMANDING OFFICER

CERTIFICATE OF APPOINTMENT

This certificate is given as recognition of
successfully meeting requirements established by the

NATIONAL RIFLE ASSOCIATION OF AMERICA
DALE C BROWN
is authorized to conduct only those training activities as prescribed in appropriate
NRA training programs for the certifications listed below.

CERTIFIED PISTOL, RIFLE, SHOTGUN, HOME FIREARM SAFETY, PERSONAL PROTECTION INSTRUCTOR

expires   MARCH 2007

Edward J. Land, Jr., Secretary

Executive Protection Institute

The Board of Directors of the Institute,
upon the recommendation of the Faculty, confer upon

Dale E. Brown

this certification as a

Personal Protection Specialist

For successful completion of the program entitled:
Providing Executive Protection. In witness whereof our
signatures are hereto affixed. Given at Berryville, Virginia
on the 18th day of   May   in the year 1996

Executive Director   Chief Instructor

DEPARTMENT OF THE ARMY

CERTIFICATE OF TRAINING

This is to certify that

PVT DALE C. BROWN

has successfully completed

End of Course Test with a Maximum score

Given at ___FLW, MO___
7 September 1989

JOHNNY T. HAMPTON SR.
CPT, IN
Commanding

DETROIT CITY COUNCIL

Testimonial Resolution

Dale Brown & Threat Management Center
Protecting, Equipping and Empowering Detroit's Communities

WHEREAS   Dale Brown, a native of Ann Arbor and former army paratrooper, is the founder of Detroit's Threat Management Center (2000), located in the Rivertown. Dale and his personnel have become recognizable through their tactical paramilitary uniform and Dale's iconic black Hummer; **and**

WHEREAS   Dale Brown model and lives by his core philosophy of heroic altruism. His personnel are required to routinely protect individuals whose lives have been threatened, such as domestic violence victims, for free and regardless of the level of risk. Threat Management Team personnel provide escorts to court, child custody transfers, and often stay with the intended victim on a 24/7 basis until the immediate threat has passed. In 2005, Dale and the Threat Management Team received an award from the Oakland County Prosecutors Office for assisting stalking victims. The Office of the Wayne County Prosecutor has given special recognition to the Threat Management Team for their voluntary protection of witnesses, domestic violence victims, and others at risk of great bodily harm; **and**

WHEREAS   Dale Brown's community service to began in the early 1990's, when he single-handedly transformed a crime ridden area near E. Jefferson and Holcomb plagued by drug dealing, robberies, assaults, home invasions and violence. With his only compensation being a room to stay, Dale confronted the drug dealers and violent criminals, persuading them to stop terrorizing residents and leave the community. Because of his courage, violent and property crime dropped more than 80 percent, and residents felt safe in their neighborhood again; **and**

WHEREAS   Dale Brown created the Survival Scouts Program in 1997 to teach youth urban survival skills, conflict avoidance and proper work ethic. Each Saturday, youth were taught Basic Self-Defense, Gunfire Evasion, Basic First Aid, Conflict Avoidance, Personal Discipline, Threat Awareness, and Problem Solving. Students were later asked to contribute to their neighborhood by cleaning local streets and parks of garbage and debris. All youth were paid for their service by Dale; **and**

WHEREAS   Dale Brown developed his own training system, called Eclectikan, built on a foundation of tactical psychology, law and skills. Dale believes that violence and conflict can be avoided by mastering non-violent physical skills to control an aggressor without resorting to injury. Dale provides free basic Eclectikan training to families every Friday night at his training center, and offers free advanced training to police officers every Monday; **NOW THEREFORE BE IT**

RESOLVED   That the Honorable Members of the Detroit City Council hereby recognize and acclaim **DALE BROWN AND THE THREAT MANAGEMENT CENTER** for their exemplary community service, unquestioned courage, and unwavering commitment to protect those most vulnerable in Detroit and the wider region.

COUNCIL PRESIDENT

COUNCIL PRESIDENT, PRO TEM   COUNCIL MEMBER

COUNCIL MEMBER   COUNCIL MEMBER

COUNCIL MEMBER   COUNCIL MEMBER

COUNCIL MEMBER   COUNCIL MEMBER

February 28, 2012
DATE

U.S. Department of Homeland Security
Fugitive Operations Group
333 Mt. Elliott Street
Detroit, Michigan 48207

U.S. Immigration
and Customs
Enforcement

August 26, 2005

To Whom It May Concern:

I have known Instructor Dale Brown for approximately one year. In that time, Detroit Fugitive Operations personnel have frequently availed themselves of the outstanding tactical training offered to sworn law enforcement officers through Threat Management Centers.

The tactical instruction taught by Instructor Brown has proven extremely useful to Fugitive Operations, with particular regard to its practicality, flexibility, and avoiding injury whenever possible while not compromising officer safety. Defensive tactics learned at Threat Management Centers were immediately applicable in the field, and have been employed many times by Fugitive Operations personnel with positive results. Additionally, the professionalism demonstrated by Instructor Brown and his staff has been second to none.

In summary, I highly recommend Instructor Brown and Threat Management Centers on both a personal and professional level.

Sincerely,

John Claypoole
Deportation Officer
DHS/ICE/DRO Fugops
333 Mt Elliot St
Detroit, MI 48207

FT. LEONARD WOOD
COMPANY E610

Brown, Cerdric L

Brown, Cleveland T

Brown, Dale C

Brown, Henry L

Brown, Jeremy A

Brown, Raymond A

Brown, Robert E
MY BATTLE BUDDY
Bucklin, Matthew W

Buffington, Bobby J

Burton, Mario D

Campbell, Keith A

Campos, Robert

Capparelli,
 Joseph J
Carey, Greg L

Castilla, Robert M

Chadwell, Brad A

Chambers, Charles T

Christian, Shawn L

Coffman, John E

Conner, Jason C

Conway, Charles L

Cooper, Arterry

Cover, Gregory A

Covington,
 Patrick S
Creed,
 Christopher

THIRD JUDICIAL CIRCUIT
OF MICHIGAN

RICHARD B. HALLORAN
CIRCUIT COURT JUDGE

COLEMAN A. YOUNG MUNICIPAL CENTER
2 WOODWARD AVENUE
DETROIT, MICHIGAN 48226-3413

(313) 224-7430
FAX (313) 224-6070

May 15, 2013

To Whom It May Concern,

As a Judge in the Family Division of Third Judicial Circuit Court in Wayne County, I am pleased to write this letter in support of the Threat Management Center.

As a Family Division Judge handling domestic relations cases with allegations of severe domestic violence between intimate partners, I see many cases where the continued safety of litigants is a serious concern. As a Family Division Judge I have specialized training in the areas of domestic, dating, and sexual violence. I strive to operate with a unique understanding of the circumstances present when there is domestic violence between parties. I am dedicated to increasing the safety of victims of domestic violence and holding batterers accountable.

Threat Management fulfills a vital need in the community by providing for the safe transportation and extraction of victims of domestic from abusive environments. Threat Management offers victims of domestic violence the personal protection and peace of mind critical to the healing process. By working with local law enforcement Threat Management helps strengthen the voices of domestic violence victims.

Over the last two years I have witnessed Threat Management working closely with our litigants and to insure the safety and security of victims of domestic violence. Threat Management has, in my humble opinion, set the standard for leadership and community outreach. In an era of shrinking police services and budget cuts to community programs, Threat Management has become a positive example of responsible corporate citizenship. By continued and active community service, Threat Management is building a safer community for all. The confidence in the personal safety Threat Management provides means victims of domestic violence will speak out against their abusers and end the cycle of violence.

Threat Management is an indispensable resource to victims of domestic violence in Southeast Michigan. As such I enthusiastically and wholly support Threat Management in its service to victims of domestic violence.

Sincerely,

Hon. Richard B. Halloran

About Dale Brown

Commander Dale C. Brown is a renowned urban survival training expert, viral internet sensation, and the founder of D.U.S.T. (Detroit Urban Survival Training) and founder and director of operations of The Detroit Management Center.

Since 1995, Commander Brown has successfully conducted workshops and training on preventive threat management which emphasizes non-violent strategies, tactics, and logistics for the public and Police.

With the tactics they applied with volunteers in the community, they were able to decrease 911 calls from 300 to 30 calls, according to the 7th precinct. This resulted in a total stop to home invasions and neighborhood murders and increased business and rental profits for the first time in 20 years in Commander Brown's east side neighborhood.

Commander Brown's YouTube channel Detroit Threat Management Center has amassed 1.82 million subscribers and garnered over 450 million views thus far.

His expertise has drawn praises from celebrities, such as DJ Khaled, Odel Beckman Jr., 2 Chains, Chainsmokers, Rick Ross, Snoop Dog and Joaquin Buckley. He's also caught the attention of media outlets and T.V. personalities, including XXL Mag, S.N.L., FOX News, Detroit Free Press, T.M.Z., CNN, HOB VICE, Rock Newman, and Adam22.

His high-profile clients include Reverend Jessie Jackson, Eric Michael Dyson, Sylvester Stallone, Jon Bon Jovi, Mary J. Blige, Ice Cube, 50 Cent, Fabulous, T.I., Lupe Fiasco, and Dick Gregory.

Please go to www.detroit-dust.com and
www.thiscansaveyourlife.com to learn more about in person
and online training.

ANTI-KILL philosophy
The belief that we must always seek a way to preserve life under
all conditions.

PROTECTION IS THE HIGHEST FORM OF LOVE
People will always protect what they truly love instinctively.

A TRUE PROTECTOR WILL ALWAYS PLACE THE
SAFETY OF OTHERS BEFORE THEIR OWN!

Our mission is to make the world a safer place for everyone,
through non-violence.

WE DO NOT STAY SAFE,
WE MAKE IT SAFE!

CPSIA information can be obtained
at www.ICGtesting.com
Printed in the USA
LVHW021050141122
732910LV00011B/202/J